King Edward V1 College
King Edward Road
Nuneaton CV11 4BE
Telephone No: 024 76328231
e-mail: learningcentres@kinged6nun.ac
Return on or before the last date stamped below

823.912
BRA

The
Connell Guide
to
Joseph Conrad's

Heart
of
Darkness

by
Graham Bradshaw

D0774036

Contents

Introduction   4

A summary of the plot   5

What is *Heart of Darkness* about?   10

How important is the narrator, Marlow?   20

Why do great critics like F.R.Leavis
think *Heart of Darkness* is flawed?   26

When and how does Marlow's "world of
straighforward facts" break down?   38

What makes Marlow come to put his
faith in Kurtz?   50

How does Marlow learn the truth about
Kurtz?   56

How does Marlow think of the jungle?   68

So what is "it"?   75

What does Kurtz mean by "The horror!
The horror!"?   84

How significant is Marlow's breakdown?   96

Why does Marlow lie to the Intended? 102

What is so distinctive about Conrad's
view of the world? 113

NOTES

At a glance: Conrad's major works   8

Is Heart of Darkness *racist?*   12

Heart of Darkness *and America*   18

Beerbohm's parody   27

Feminist assaults   29

The primary narrator   30

Ivory   34

Niggers   46

Ten facts about Heart of Darkness   64

Conrad, Hardy and pessimism   86

Fin-de-siècle   114

A short chronology   126

Bibliography   128

Introduction

Conrad finished *Heart of Darkness* on 9th February, 1899 and it was originally published in three parts in that important organ of Victorian high culture, *Blackwood's Magazine*, Part One appearing in the 1,000th issue. Three years then passed before it was republished in book form as the second story in the collection *Youth: A Narrative, and Two Other Stories*. While "Youth" has always been highly regarded, the third story in this volume, "The End of the Tether", has had little critical attention – even Conrad himself said in later life he didn't think it likely he'd read it again.

But *Heart of Darkness* had an impact as powerful as any long short story, or short novel ever written – it is only 38,000 words. It quickly became, and has remained, Conrad's most famous work and has been regarded by many in America, if not elsewhere, as his greatest work. Exciting and profound, lucid and bewildering, and written with an exuberance which sometimes seems at odds with its subject matter, it has influenced writers as diverse as T.S.Eliot (in *The Four Quartets* and *The Waste Land*), Graham Greene (*The Third Man, A Burnt-Out Case*), William Golding (*The Inheritors*) and Ngugi wa Thiong'o (*A Grain of Wheat*). It has also inspired, among others, Orson Welles, who made two radio versions the second of which, in 1945, depicted Kurtz as a forerunner of

Adolf Hitler, and Francis Ford Coppola who turned it into the film *Apocalypse Now*.

More critical attention has probably been paid to it, per word, than to any other modern prose work. It has also become a text about which, as the late Frank Kermode once complained, interpreters feel licensed to say absolutely anything. Why? What is it about *Heart of Darkness* that has captivated critics and readers for so long and caused so many millions of words to be written about it? And why has its peculiarly dark and intense vision of life so frequently been misunderstood?

A summary of the plot

The story opens at dusk on the deck of a cruising yawl, the Nellie, moored in the Thames estuary. An unnamed narrator sits with four friends, one of whom, Marlow, begins to tell the clearly traumatic story of his journey on another river – in Africa. After a number of false starts, Marlow describes how he goes to Brussels where a trading company recommended by his aunt appoints him as a riverboat captain in the Congo. He travels by ship to take up his post and on arrival is disgusted by what he sees of the greed of the ivory traders and the brutal way in which they exploit the natives.

At the company's Outer Station he hears about the most remarkable and successful ivory trader of all, Mr Kurtz, who is stationed in the heart of the country. Marlow sets out to find him, first making an arduous cross-country trek to the company's Central Station. There, however, he finds that the steamboat he is to command on the journey upriver to find Kurtz has been mysteriously wrecked. He hears that Kurtz is seriously ill and believes the manager and others at the Central Station – jealous of his success – are plotting to deprive him of supplies and medicine in the hope that he will die. Marlow takes Kurtz to be an idealist with higher and nobler motives than his fellow traders and is anxious to meet him. He also becomes convinced his departure from the Central Station is being deliberately delayed.

Finally, after frustrating months of repairs to the steamboat, he sets off on the eight-week journey upriver to find Kurtz. He feels growing dread. The journey is "like travelling back to the earliest beginnings of the world". As the boat draws near to the Inner Station it is attacked by tribesmen and the helmsman is killed. When Marlow arrives he meets a half-mad young Russian, who tells him of Kurtz's brilliance and the semi-divine power he wields over the natives.

Marlow, however, soon realizes that Kurtz has achieved his status by indulging in barbaric rites: a row of severed heads on stakes round his hut testify to the way this educated and once civilised man has achieved his ascendancy. He is now dying. As Marlow attempts to move him back down river, Kurtz tries to justify his actions, then, before dying, utters his famous and cryptic last words: " The horror! The horror!" After Kurtz's death, Marlow has a breakdown and remembers little of his journey home. A year later, he visits Kurtz's fiancée in Brussels. Faced with her grief he can't bring himself to tell her the truth. Instead he simply tells her that the last words spoken by Kurtz were "your name".

John Malkovich and Iman as Kurtz and Black Beauty in Nicholas Roeg's 1993 film adaptation

AT A GLANCE:
CONRAD'S MAJOR WORKS

THE NIGGER OF THE NARCISSUS: A TALE OF THE SEA (1897)

Conrad's first great novel. The story of a West Indian sailor of African descent, who falls ill during a voyage from Bombay to London on the merchant ship Narcissus.

YOUTH (1898)

A semi-autobiographical short story based on Conrad's first ill-fated journey to Bangkok, first, published in 1902 as part of the same volume that contained *Heart of Darkness* (with which it shares its fictional narrator, Marlow).

LORD JIM (1900)

Also narrated by Marlow. Jim – one of Conrad's most enigmatic figures; we never learn his surname – is first mate on the Patna. In a moment of weakness, he abandons ship when it runs aground. Publicly disgraced, he is sent to a fictional island near China where he becomes a local hero, falls in love and finally dies for his honour.

NOSTROMO (1904)

Conrad's greatest novel. Charles Gould inherits a silver mine from his father in the fictional South American republic of Costaguana, which he reopens. But the wealth he creates leads only to corruption and violence. Gould entrusts his silver to the "incorruptible" Nostromo, who hides it. But this is

Conrad, and no one is incorruptible. Nostromo meets his death when, attempting to recover more of the silver for himself, he is mistaken for a trespasser.

THE SECRET AGENT: A SIMPLE TALE (1907)

Conrad's only London novel. Adolf Verloc, owner of a seedy pornographic shop in Soho and member of a largely ineffectual anarchist terrorist group, is employed as a secret agent by an unnamed foreign country and instructed to blow up the Greenwich Observatory. Verloc's brother-in-law is killed by the bomb, which prompts Verloc to confess to his wife, who goes mad and stabs him to death.

UNDER WESTERN EYES (1911)

A young Russian student, Razumov, finds a fellow student, Victor Haldin, hiding in his apartment. Haldin confesses to a political assassination, and asks for Razumov's help. Instead, Razumov goes to the police, and Haldin is hanged. Meanwhile, Haldin's sister receives a letter from Haldin saying Razumov has helped him. Razumov travels to Switzerland, where he falls in love with her and ends up confessing what he has done.

CHANCE (1913)

The fourth and last of Conrad's stories to feature Marlow, this is the novel that, finally, brought him commercial success and turned him into a celebrity, selling 13,000 copies in its first two years in Britain and 20,000 in its first seven months in America. Unusually for Conrad, it has a female central character – Flora de Barral, whose father is bankrupt and imprisoned – and a happy ending.

What is *Heart of Darkness* about?

The English critic F.R. Leavis, the American critic Lionel Trilling, and the American-Palestinian critic Edward Said – three of the most important and influential critics of Conrad – all answered this question in very different, sometimes incompatible ways. That could be taken as a warning that there is no simple, timeless or final answer to the question of what *Heart of Darkness* is about, and these three critics didn't even agree whether it was an "exasperating", "badly marred" work (Leavis), or a "very great work" (Trilling), or Conrad's "very greatest work" (Said). But the differences between these critics are also instructive, and help us to see how the novel engages the reader in two ways.

On the one hand it is a courageous and passionate attack on imperialism. On the other it is an early and extraordinarily original example of what came to be called "modernism", both in the complexity of its narrative method and in its urgent existentialist concern with how we are to live and with what we can live by in an unaccommodating world that is hostile or, at best, indifferent to human values.

There is, of course, no contradiction between saying that *Heart of Darkness* is both an early modernist classic and a powerful political assault on the ideology of imperialism. James Joyce's *Ulysses* (1922), arguably the greatest of all modernist novels, is also vehemently political in its attack on the two foreign powers that, in Joyce's view, had blighted Irish history, namely England and the Roman Catholic Church.

Among those who have done most to highlight the political aspect of Conrad's work is the Palestinian-American, Edward Said. Conrad was the writer who meant most to Said during his immensely productive life as a critic and political activist, and the book which meant most to him was *Heart of Darkness*. In *Conrad in the Twenty-First Century*, a volume dedicated to the memory of Said, who died in 2003, the editors argue that he

> changed the landscape of British and Anglophone literary studies by moving Conrad and the issues of imperialism foregrounded in his writings to its center, reversing the metropolitan biases and blindness of the Western canon as previously constructed, and opening the door to global and postcolonial articulations of literary and cultural history.

Certainly, Said "foregrounded" the "issues of imperialism" that had not been addressed in the essays of some of the great early critics of Conrad, like Trilling and Leavis, although it is not so certain that Conrad himself "foregrounded" them "in his writings".

That *Heart of Darkness* is fiercely anti-imperialist, there is no doubt. As Patrick Brantlinger observes in his magnificent study, *Rule of Darkness,* it is a "measure of Conrad's achievement" that "almost no other work of British fiction written before World War One is critical of imperialism".

Conrad's attitude stemmed from the six months he spent in the Congo in 1890, where he was appalled by what he saw in the territory that King Leopold II of Belgium – his ultimate employer – treated as his private domain. In his essay "Geography and the Explorers", the novelist describes what Leopold was doing to the "Belgian"

IS *HEART OF DARKNESS* RACIST?

In 1975, the Nigerian novelist, Chinua Achebe, famously asserted that *Heart of Darkness* reveals Conrad to be "a bloody racist" who had "a problem with niggers". The blacks, he says, are dehumanized and degraded or shown as grotesques in a howling mob: they are denied speech or granted it only to condemn themselves from their own mouths.

Few postcolonial writers have shared these views. Francis B. Singh, for example, says that the story is vulnerable in some respects – he objects to the association of Africans with supernatural evil in the

Congo as "the vilest scramble for loot that ever disfigured the history of human conscience and geographical exploration". In *Heart of Darkness*, Conrad's immediate concern in political and historical terms was the behaviour of Leopold II, but that his target was broader than that is evident from the way he compares Leopold with British and Roman imperialists and gives the ruthless ivory trader Kurtz a mixed European background to reinforce the idea that the whole continent was involved in the plunder of Africa. As his narrator Marlow laconically puts it:

The conquest of the earth, which mostly means the taking it away from those who have a different complexion or slightly flatter noses

scene where a sinister figure wearing horns attends one of Kurtz's nocturnal rituals. But he says the story should remain in "the canon of works indicting colonialism".

Cedric Watts makes a good defence of Conrad. He takes issue with Achebe's assertion that Africa is depicted by Conrad as "a place of negations" so as to emphasize "Europe's own state of spiritual grace", pointing out that Marlow's tale – and it is Marlow who is speaking – challenges this contrast in all kinds of ways.

As Africa is to present-day Europeans, Marlow suggests, England was to Roman colonists. When he describes depopulated regions of Africa, Marlow reflects that the Kentish countryside would also become rapidly depopulated if it were invaded by heavily armed strangers. The sound of *than ourselves, is not a pretty thing when you look into it too much.*

Be it Belgian or British, imperial conquest is always, Marlow maintains, about tearing "treasure out of the bowels" of other peoples' land, "with no more moral purpose at the back of it than there is in burglars breaking into a safe".

One might want to argue in historical and even in moral terms, and Marlow himself seems disposed to believe (as indeed did Conrad), that what the British were doing on some of "the red spots of the map" – in India, for example, after if not before the 1857 Indian mutiny – was at least less atrocious than what the Belgians were

drums in the jungle as "perhaps... as profound a meaning as the sound of bells in a Christian country". The whites of the Eldorado Expedition ride their donkeys into the jungle, and Marlow comments: "Long afterwards the news came that all the donkeys were dead. I know nothing as to the fate of the less valuable animals." (If he had referred to blacks rather than whites as "less valuable animals" critics would have cited this as evidence of racism.) Kurtz, we are told, is not worth "the life we lost in getting to him": the life of the black helmsman. The cannibal crew evinces remarkable restraint; it is Kurtz, the European, who "lacked all restraint in the gratification of his various lusts", and who, it is implied, may have drunk blood and consumed human flesh.

Given that it was written in the heyday of Victorian imperialism, *Heart* doing in the Congo, or that British colonial administrators like Leonard Woolf, Joyce Cary or George Orwell were more "principled" than Leopold II's rapacious agents in the Congo. And so they were.

But Woolf, Cary and Orwell all quit, after concluding that such arguments involve splitting hairs. In the end, *Heart of Darkness* suggests, nothing can justify imperialism, and although it has often been called an "ambivalent" text, it is not ambivalent on that crucial issue. It deconstructs every possible justification for imperialism, from the arguments about "mutual benefit" and "the white man's burden", to the assumptions of those who believed that they belonged to a Chosen Race

---

of Darkness seems extraordinarily progessive in it's attitudes. Indeed, as Watts reminds us, the intense animus Conrad feels against the European "pilgrims" can "make us briefly forget the enduring technological accomplishments (the railways, the roads, the establishment of new townships) which, for all the depredations, changed the face of Africa". Nor does Marlow say anything about the atrocities committed by black imperialists or the slave-trading conducted on a large scale by Arabs and their local accomplices in Africa. Finally, the only group of people in the story shown to be happy with their environment in *Heart of Darkness* is not European: it is the singing blacks who, with "wild vitality" and "intense energy of movement", paddle their boat through the coastal surf. "They" – unlike the whites – "wanted not excuse for being there".◆

– from Ruskin and so many 19th century Englishmen to the Americans who rattled on about belonging to "God's Own Country".*

True as all this is, however, it is hard to justify the assumption which lies behind the American volume, *Conrad in the Twenty-First Century*, that his anti-imperialism is at the core of his writing. There is a new though largely "unstated" 21st century "consensus" about Conrad, says J. Hillis Miller in the book's Foreward: all the essays, like him, are "thoroughly politicised", and all "are unanimous in not taking seriously any 'metaphysical' dimension of Conrad's work".

This may be an accurate assessment of the essays, but it is a bizarre claim. As Said himself acknowledged in his last formal interview, Conrad's concerns were always broader than those of his more partisan critics. Indeed, said Said, Conrad didn't believe in political action of any kind. "I think he thought it was all vain... I've been attracted to lost causes all my life – and Conrad is the great illuminator of that particular. But he does it from an ironic and disengaged and quite sceptical view". To Said, Conrad was

> a pessimist in the way that Nietzsche is a
> pessimist... the big difference between Conrad
> and me in the end – and this is true of *Nostromo* as

*See Rudyard Kipling's 1899 poem "The White Man's Burden", subtitled "The United States and The Philippine Islands".

well as *Heart of Darkness* – is that politically for Conrad there are no real alternatives. And I disagree with him: there's always an alternative... [But] Conrad is just incapable of that kind of constitutive hope, and I would even call it frivolous to ascribe it to him.

Conrad's pessimistic sense that human nature is largely corruptible and fallible, says the British critic Cedric Watts, led him "to the humanitarian insight that since the 'civilised' people are not likely to be much better (if at all) than the so-called 'inferior races', we might as well leave remote nations alone". But, as Watts says, and as this book will show, Conrad's preoccupations in *Heart of Darkness* go well beyond the destructive aspects of imperialism.

Lionel Trilling talks of the book's "strange and terrible message of ambivalence towards the life of civilization". Many commentators have remarked that Marlow's journey into the interior of Africa is, at the same time, an interior journey: as D.C.R.A. Goonetilleke puts it, "at a symbolic level the journey into the Congo becomes also a journey into the depths of man's unconscious, revealed in all its darkness". Conrad was never interested in Freud, but he took a similar view of man's destructive tendencies and the same conviction that culture is based on repression and restraint, and the maintenance of illusions.

In one of many letters to his friend, the Scottish socialist Cunninghame Graham, Conrad wrote, with slightly theatrical despair, of the universe as a soulless mechanism determining human lives:

There is – let us say – a machine. It evolved itself (I am severely scientific) out of a chaos of scraps of iron and behold! – it knits. I am horrified at the horrible work and stand appalled. I feel it ought to embroider – but it goes on knitting... And the most withering thought is that the infamous thing has made itself without thought, without conscience, without foresight, without eyes, without heart. It is

HEART OF DARKNESS AND AMERICA

For many years, *Heart of Darkness* was the literary text most frequently set in courses in American universities and colleges of education. The reason for this was political.

Completed in February 1899, it was an indictment of British and European imperialism; in *Nostromo*, on the other hand, which Conrad finished in late 1903, and which he himself and many British and European critics regarded as his greatest novel, he was presciently concerned with emergent, soon to be dominant, American imperialism. Not surprisingly, Americans found the earlier work more congenial, although some critics, including Lionel Trilling, felt Conrad had not a tragic accident – and it has happened. The last drop of bitterness is in the suspicion that you can't even smash it....

It knits us in and it knits us out. It has knitted time, space, pain, death, corruption, despair and all the illusions – and nothing matters. I'll admit however that to look at the remorseless process is sometimes amusing.

Conrad's story is about much more than colonialism. His heart of darkness is not just in Africa. It is also in us.

---

gone far enough in his indictment of the British. The political reason for *Heart of Darkness's* popularity took a knock in 1975 when the Nigerian novelist Chinua Achebe denounced it as a "racist" work; Achebe's views were not widely shared, but America's centres of higher education duly took note.

The belief that *Heart of Darkness* is a greater work than *Nostromo* lingers on in American campuses, however, and was reinforced by the publication in 2003 of *Conrad in the Twenty-First Century*. What is most striking about this re-assessment is that it is dominated by American critics. There is an irony in this. The sweeping, seemingly automatic exclusion of all non-American critics – of British critics like Cedric Watts, and even of European critics like Zdzislaw Najder – is itself, of course, a kind of cultural imperialism of the kind Trilling might have condemned had it been practised by any country other than the United States. ◆

How important is the narrator, Marlow?

Conrad once said that *Heart of Darkness* and his earlier story, "An Outpost of Progress", were "all the loot" that he "brought back from the centre of Africa". The relationship between "An Outpost of Progress", which was first published in July 1897, the year of Queen Victoria's Diamond Jubilee, and *Heart of Darkness* is best suggested by his comment in a letter to his publisher, T. Fisher Unwin. "It is a story of the Congo," he writes, set in "a lonely station on the Kassai", although the "exact locality is not mentioned". He then adds:

> All the bitterness of those days, all my puzzled wonder as to the meaning of all I saw – all my indignation at masquerading philanthropy – have been with me again, while I wrote.

Like Robert Louis Stevenson's earlier, very powerful *The Beach at Falesá*, Conrad's story shows how the so-called emissaries of "progress" were often men of poor character who could find no better employment at home, so went to the tropics, and then went to seed. The unnamed narrator rails against the self-justifying assurances of this "civilized crowd":

Few men realise that their life, the very essence of their character, their capabilities and their audacities, are only the expression of their belief in the safety of their surroundings. The courage, the composure, the confidence; the emotions and principles; every great and insignificant thought belongs not to the individual but to the crowd: to the crowd that believes blindly in the irresistible force of its institutions and of its morals, in the power of its police and of its opinion. But the contact with pure unmitigated savagery, with primitive nature man, brings sudden and profound trouble into the heart.

In *Heart of Darkness*, we more than once see Marlow flaring up when he supposes that a similarly blind belief in the safety of their surroundings accounts for his old friends' inability to understand his story:

You can't understand. How could you? – with solid pavement under your feet, surrounded by kind neighbours ready to cheer you or to fall on you, stepping delicately between the butcher and the policeman, in the holy terror of scandal and gallows and lunatic asylum.

But although the passage from "An Outpost of Progress" anticipates *Heart of Darkness* in this respect, it also shows how the earlier story is different. The frequent comments of its unnamed narrator are so explicit as to be clumsily didactic, whereas Marlow is uncertain how to tell his story, because he is painfully unsure what his experience signifies.

Through his use of a protagonist who is also the narrator, Conrad gives *Heart of Darkness* a depth and a perspective which "An Outpost of Progress" lacks. As Marlow tells his story to his old friends on the cruising yawl Nellie, he is reliving and revising it – or revising the story he had originally told to himself. Everything that is achieved through this intensely dramatised narration would be lost if there were some omniscient narrator who could explain to us what Kurtz's last words "really" meant, or why Marlow's breakdown lasted for more than a year. [See The primary narrator, p.30]

Conrad had first introduced Marlow in "Youth", written earlier than *Heart of Darkness* and published in the same volume of stories in 1902. Both begin with the same group of five old friends assembling for a kind of reunion on the cruising yawl, Nellie. Because it is so important that Marlow tells his stories to this group of friends with the immediacy of live speech, both stories are launched and also closed by the primary narrator – one of the five friends – before Marlow takes over.

In "Youth", the volume's title story, the primary

narrator is little more than a peg on which to hang the tale. The assembled "fellows" – who "all began life in the merchant service" and were united by the "strong bond of the sea" – are named as "a director of companies, an accountant, a lawyer, Marlow, and myself".

"Youth" is like one of Blake's Songs of Innocence compared to the much darker Song of Experience that is *Heart of Darkness*. It is a simple, warmly nostalgic story of dangers overcome in which the 47-year-old Marlow recalls an early episode in his own life, when he faced dangers that didn't come close to destroying him. *Heart of Darkness,* on the other hand, as Conrad observed in a 1917 "Author's Note", is "more ambitious in its scope and longer in its telling", and is "obviously written in another mood... I won't characterize the mood precisely, but anybody can see that it is anything but the mood of wistful regret, of reminiscent tenderness."

When the same group of friends reassembles in *Heart of Darkness* they are identified – not by Marlow but by the primary narrator – with more accusatory, Dickensian capitals: they have turned into the "Director of Companies", the "Lawyer" and the "Accountant". It is an early sign of the story's effect on the primary narrator: they have become Pillars of Society, and of course this gives point to the growled protest one of them later makes, which is all the more consummately ironic because the speaker (unidentified) is not conscious of irony: "Try to be civil, Marlow." Marlow offers a half-hearted or sarcastic apology: "I beg your pardon. I forgot the heartache which makes up the rest of the price." But later, when someone sighs in a "beastly way" and mutters "Absurd", the irritated Marlow fills his pipe and then assails the whole company:

> *This is the worst of trying to tell... Here you all are, each moored with two good addresses, like a hulk with two anchors, a butcher round one corner, a policeman round another, excellent appetites, and temperature normal – you hear – normal from year's end to year's end. And you say, Absurd! Absurd be – exploded! Absurd!*

The primary narrator is more chauvinistic than Marlow, launching the story with a sonorously cadenced hymn to "the great spirit of the past" which presents the kind of vision of Britain reminiscent of children's history books with uplifting titles like *Our Island's Story*.

> *We looked at the venerable stream not in the vivid flush of a short day that comes and departs for ever, but in the august light of abiding memories. And indeed nothing is easier for a man who has, as the phrase goes, 'followed the sea' with reverence and affection, than to evoke*

*the great spirit of the past upon the lower
reaches of the Thames. The tidal current runs to
and fro in its unceasing service, crowded with
memories of men and ships it had borne to the
rest of home or to the battles of the sea. It had
known and served all the men of whom the
nation is proud, from Sir Francis Drake to Sir
John Franklin, knights all, titled and untitled –
the great knights-errant of the sea. It had borne
all the ships whose names are like jewels
flashing in the nights of time, from the Golden
Hind returning with her round flanks full of
treasure... to the Erebus and Terror, bound on
other conquests – and that never returned. It
had known the ships and the men... Hunters for
gold or pursuers of fame, they had all gone out
on the stream, bearing the sword, and often the
torch, messengers of the night within the land,
bearers of a spark from the sacred fire.*

Of course the primary narrator is also establishing
the setting, in the Nellie where the friends sit
together, each lost in his own thoughts but
seeming to share the charged silence – the kind of
moment when the French say, very beautifully,
that an angel is passing. Each time we read *Heart
of Darkness* this poetic summoning casts its spell,
and even in a first reading we feel the Thames
haunted by different phases of the island's history.
Marlow breaks this charged silence when he

"suddenly" says: "And this also has been one of the dark places of the earth".

Marlow's next words suggest that the primary narrator's patriotic hymn, with its tribute to the "great knights-errant of the sea" who sailed out, "bearing the sword, and often the torch", and "a spark from the sacred fire" has been spoken, at least in part: "I was thinking of very old times, when the Romans first came here, nineteen hundred years ago – the other day... Lights came out of this river since – you say Knights? Yes, but..." It is as though Marlow has somehow heard the primary narrator's written version of the British imperialist vision, and is then prompted to tell his own story, which savagely undermines this vision.

Why do great critics like F.R. Leavis think *Heart of Darkness* is flawed?

In a famous essay in his book, *Abinger Harvest*, E.M. Forster complains about a "central obscurity" in Conrad's writings. "What is so elusive about him is that he is always promising to make some general philosophical statement about the universe, and then refraining with a gruff disclaimer..." Forster suggests that Conrad "is misty in the middle as well as at the edges, that the secret casket of his genius contains a vapour rather than a jewel; and that we needn't try and write him down philosophically, because there is, in this direction, nothing to write".

In 1941, F.R. Leavis published his sharply diagnostic account of *Heart of Darkness* in the

BEERBOHM'S PARODY

Sometimes, Conrad's stylistic excesses invited parody. He himself acknowledged as much when he publicly conceded that he had been "most agreeably guyed" by Max Beerbohm in *A Christmas Garland* (1912). Beerbohm's story "The Feast" is an affectionate parody of a Conrad story called "The Lagoon", and the following passage suggests how Beerbohm's main target—which he hit so brilliantly—was the younger Conrad's combination of annihilating Schopehauerian pessimism and tropical prolixity:

The roofs of the congested trees, writhing in some kind of agony private and eternal, made tenebrous and shifty silhouettes against the sky, like shapes cut out of black paper by a maniac who pushes them with his thumb this way and that, irritably, on a concave surface of blue steel. Resin oozed unseen from the upper branches to the trunks swathed in creepers that clutched and interlocked with tendrils venomous, frantic and faint. Down below, by force of habit, the lush herbage went through the farce of growth - that farce old and screaming, whose trite end is decomposition. Within the hut the form of the white man, corpulent and pale, was covered with a mosquito-net that was itself illusory like everything else, only more so. ◆

Cambridge journal Scrutiny, an essay later reprinted with Leavis's later *Scrutiny* essays in *The Great Tradition.* * For Leavis, Conrad's greatest novels assured his place in the "great tradition", but he insisted on the urgent need to discriminate between Conrad's "classical work" and more uneven works like *Heart of Darkness*, that revealed "a disconcerting weakness or vice".

Echoing E.M. Forster's exasperated view, Leavis observed that the greatness attributed to Conrad "tended to be identified with an imputed profundity, and that this profundity was not what it was taken to be, but quite other, and the reverse of a strength". Leavis then set out to show "how *Heart of Darkness* is marred".

Leavis allows that parts of it show "Conrad's art at his best", but complains about his intrusive comments and "adjectival insistence":

Hadn't he, we find ourselves asking, overworked

---

*This was an important but controversial book; many reviewers and later critics protested that Leavis's concept of a "great tradition" was too narrow. Jane Austen, George Eliot, Henry James and Conrad – "among the very greatest novelists in the language" – were "in", and so, of course, was D.H. Lawrence, the novelist who mattered most to Leavis: Leavis's essays on Lawrence, which became the basis of his book, D.H. Lawrence: Novelist (1953), had first appeared in Scrutiny in the late 1930s, when very few people regarded Lawrence as a great novelist. But other novelists were "out", including Fielding, Dickens and James Joyce; Leavis later revised his startlingly low estimate of Dickens, but not of Joyce.

"inscrutable', "inconceivable", "unspeakable" and that kind of word already? – yet still they recur. Is anything added to the oppressive mysteriousness of the jungle by such sentences as: "It was the stillness of an implacable force brooding over an inscrutable intention"? The same vocabulary, the same adjectival insistence upon inexpressible and incomprehensible mystery, is applied to the evocation of human potentialities and spiritual horrors; to magnifying a thrilled sense of the unspeakable potentialities of the human soul. The actual effect is not to magnify but to muffle.

FEMINIST ASSAULTS

Predictably, Conrad has been attacked as a male chauvinist. "The woman reader," says Nina Straus, one of many feminist critics to take issue with *Heart of Darkness*, "is in the position to insist that Marlow's cowardice consists of his inability to face the dangerous self that is the form of his own masculinist vulnerability: his own complicity in the racist, sexist, imperialistic, and finally libidinally satisfying world he has inhabited with Kurtz."

It is true that the world of *Heart of Darkness* is predominantly male, and that Marlow's views on women are old-fashioned, even quaint. But it is worth mentioning, as feminist critics rarely do, that Conrad was a supporter of female suffrage, and that in 1910 he signed an open letter to the Prime Minister, Herbert Asquith, advocating votes for women. ◆

Leavis goes on to quote further passages that show how, in his view, Conrad "feels that there is, or ought to be, some horror, some significance he has yet to bring out", and his damning conclusion is that

> Conrad must here stand convicted of borrowing the arts of the magazine writer (who has borrowed his, shall we say, from Kipling and Poe) in order to impose on his readers and on himself, for thrilled response, a "significance" that is merely an emotional insistence on the presence of what he can't produce. The insistence betrays the absence, the willed "intensity", the nullity. He is intent on

THE PRIMARY NARRATOR

There is no "omniscient" narrator in *Heart of Darkness*. Conrad needs another narrator who can recall and record, word for word, exactly what Marlow said. Not only that: Conrad needed his primary narrator to provide what were in effect stage directions.

In this, Henry James – whom Conrad usually addressed in his letters as "Cher Maître" or "Dear Master" – provided a useful model. James's use of the "scenic method" followed his painful failure to write a successful play (a lucrative sideline for 19th-century novelists). He would present one character's "point of view", like that of the child Maisie in *What Maisie Knew*, and otherwise restrict himself to what he called "the scenic method" by making a virtue out of not knowing what he means.

But when Leavis writes "he" in that last sentence, he means Conrad, although not one of the passages that prompt his angry diagnostic protests is an authorial "comment", as Leavis constantly assumes.

The passages in question are all spoken (not written) by Marlow, who is both the narrator and the protagonist. In so simply identifying Conrad with Marlow, Leavis was making what J. Hillis Miller calls an "elementary reading mistake". D.H. Lawrence had made the same mistake in his 1913 review (a review which Leavis greatly admired) of

---

showing only what t a theatrical audience could either hear or see. So, for example, if a character became agitated, that might be suggested by the way he found and lit a cigarette or, like Marlow, fussed with his pipe and got cross when the "match went out".

In other words, Conrad's primary narrator was also valuable in that he could describe – like Bernard Shaw in his copious stage directions – the charged silences and dramatically revealing moments in Marlow's dramatic narrative when he broke off and asked someone to "Pass the claret", or suddenly exploded with frustration or rage, assailing his old friends (among them the primary narrator) like some angry Samson Agonistes who suddenly wants to pull down these infuriating and damnable Pillars of Society: "This is the worst of trying to tell... Here you all are, each moored with two good addresses..." ◆

Thomas Mann's *Death in Venice*, which turned into an assault on "the Thomas Mann of fifty-three", mistakenly identifying the tale's author with its narrator-protagonist,

Both Leavis, who was arguably the greatest 20th century English critic, and Lawrence, who was almost certainly the greatest 20th-century English novelist, were oddly unresponsive to the narrative complexities and formal experimentation that were an important feature of modernist writing. This helps to explain their shared dislike of Joyce – and of Flaubert, who mattered very much to Joyce, Henry James and Conrad. Leavis frequently quotes Lawrence's famous maxim "Never trust the teller, trust the tale", but, in their respective accounts of *Heart of Darkness* and *Death in Venice*, both Leavis and Lawrence based their impatiently and impertinently diagnostic criticism of the tellers on readings of the tales that were woefully indifferent to how the tales are told*.

In few stories does the way the tale is told matter as much as it does in *Heart of Darkness*. It is as much, if not more, the tale of Marlow's

---

*Lawrence's dismissive comments on Joyce ("a clumsy ulla putrida"), Proust ("water-jelly", "masturbation self-enclosure"), Conrad ("snivel in a wet hanky", "giving in before you start"), and other modernists are no less impatiently diagnostic than his diagnosis of Mann and characterise his concern to separate the "quick" from the "dead", so as to move on quickly.

agonised attempt to come to terms with his terrible experience in Africa as it is about the experience itself, and the expressions Leavis objects to are part of this attempt as Marlow vainly seeks to make sense of what he's been through. He is trying to find the words to describe something which, to him, seems beyond the power of words to describe, and to accuse Conrad of straining for effect, as Leavis does, is ridiculous. One of the themes of *Heart of Darkness*, though this seems lost on Leavis, is the inadequacy of language to represent reality.

Indeed to accuse Conrad of "a kind of self-indulgent negative whimsy" as Leavis does, says Valentine Cunningham, is to miss the entire point of his story. *Heart of Darkness* is in effect a rejection of the traditional, 19th century mode of story-telling. "The protagonists in most traditional novels... are breezy with confidence that something positive is to be gained by their time in the narration. They're on a kind of voyage of discovery." Like some of Henry James's later characters, however, Conrad's Marlow experiences something which shakes his knowledge and leaves him feeling not less but more uncertain about the world. *Heart of Darkness*, says Cunningham

> ...is the busiest of refusing, sceptical, self-emptying texts. It steadily inducts the reader into negativity, blankness, crypticity... It's full of narrative failure

– the failure of narrators, of narrating, and so, it's possible to argue, of narrativity itself.

The endless puzzles, gaps and ambiguities in the text, Cunningham goes on,

bring vividly home the modern collapse of language into ambivalence, puzzle and silence, and so illustrate the 20th century novel's widespread sense of the difficulty of keeping up story-telling, old-fashioned subjects, character and reference, the old assurances about the selfhood of persons and narratives.

IVORY

Though F.R. Leavis complained of the abstract language in *Heart of Darkness*, Conrad said, in one of his letters to Cunninghame Graham, that the story began not "with an abstract notion" but with "definite images". There are plenty such images – all those metallic objects in the jungle, for example: the shells lobbed into the bush, the nuts and bolts, the decaying boiler, the rusted steamboat. "The profusion of metallic and mechanical images," writes Frederick Karl, "indicates that resistant objects have superseded softness, flexibililty, humanity itself; that, clearly, one must become an object, tough and durable, in order to survive". One interesting example is the Huntley & Palmer's biscuit-tin. "She rang under my feet like an empty Huntley & Palmer (sic) biscuit-tin kicked along a gutter," says Marlow. Huntley & Palmers biscuit

Since Leavis never saw the need to distinguish between Conrad and Marlow, he never saw the need to distinguish between Marlow the narrator and Marlow the protagonist. Nor did other great critics, like Trilling and Said. Yet the so-called "narrative gap" in *Heart of Darkness* is crucial to understanding it.

In classic 19th century first-person narratives like *Great Expectations* and *Jane Eyre*, which all begin with the protagonist as a child, the narrative gap between the protagonist and the narrator gradually closes as we read: in these stories the narrating voice is clearly adult, but the narrative

tins were everywhere in the empire, Valentine Cunningham reminds us, and "stood for one of the most extraordinary and far-flung triumphs of colonialist marketing and propaganda that Victorian Britain knew".

But the most important object – the one, as Karl puts it, that best sums up the sense of "human waste" pervading the story – is, of course, ivory. Like the equally significant silver in *Nostromo*, it is an object for the rich: for decoration or for piano keys. The lives being sacrificed in Africa are being sacrificed for something without real utility or human value. In a way, says Karl, ivory is "like art, a social luxury, and it is for art that the Congo is plundered and untold numbers slaughtered brutally... Possibly Kurtz's artistic propensities... make him so contemptuous of individual lives; for art and life have always warred. In the name of art (pyramids, churches, tombs, monuments, palaces), how many have died gone without, worked as slaves? Traditionally, beauty for the few is gained with the blood of the many." ◆

shows how the protagonist, who is at first still a child, gradually turns into the narrator whose voice we are hearing from the start. Such structures admit a good deal of subtlety and suspense, as the opening chapters of *Great Expectations* show: we wonder what has happened to Pip as a child that has made him sound so unhappy and punishingly self-critical as an adult. In *Great Expectations*, as in *Jane Eyre*, the gap between protagonist and narrator is in effect closed by the end of the novel.

In *Heart of Darkness*, however, the narrative gap is never closed. We never learn what has happened to Marlow between the final pages of the book and the opening pages when he begins to tell his story. The experiences he recounts end with him in Brussels, still badly affected by the complete, nearly fatal mental and physical breakdown he had suffered in Africa, but the book begins, years later, when Marlow tells his friends of these experiences and when we first see him "sitting cross-legged fore aft" and seeming less English than Oriental:

> *He had sunken cheeks, a yellow complexion, a straight back, an ascetic aspect, and, with his arms dropped, the palms of both hand outwards, resembled an idol.*

Opposite: Joseph Conrad, c. 1923

The effect of this is to underline the life-changing nature of Marlow's time in Africa. What has happened to him is so shocking, so terrible that he has never recovered from it and never managed to reconcile himself to it. It has disrupted his life to such an extent that it has, in effect, made him into a different person – and made it impossible for him to see his life as one continuous whole in which each event leads to the next, as is the case with, say, Pip or Jane Eyre. Marlow's experience has detached him not just from the everyday world but, in a sense, from himself. The narrative gap between the young and the middle-aged Marlow is not just unclosed; it is uncloseable. Failure to understand this gap, like failure to attend to the fact that it is Marlow's voice we are hearing, makes it hard to appreciate the subtlety of Conrad's art in *Heart of Darkness*.

When and how does Marlow's "world of straightforward facts" break down?

Ted Hughes once remarked that when a man grows older and has carried out his "biological function" – after finding his mate, having his children and establishing himself in his world – he can find himself troubled and bewildered by the sense that "Nature" has somehow now "finished with him" and "moved on" to the next generation. A greater "inwardness" may then follow, like an invasion, but there is a correspondingly profound change in the man's relation to the world "outside", the world of Nature and Society.

Hughes's remarks concern what is popularly called the mid-life crisis. This kind of crisis, which the 40-year-old Hughes presented so movingly in *Cave Birds* (1975), was also the starting point for the journey in Dante's great medieval poem *La Divina Commedia* or *Divine Comedy*: "Nel mezzo del cammin di nostra vita / Mi ritrovai per una selva oscura" – Midway in the journey of our life, I found myself in a dark or obscure wood.

Although Conrad's Marlow never marries or has children, Ted Hughes's remarks about a mid-life crisis seem no less suggestive in his case. If we are reading *Heart of Darkness* as the second story that Marlow tells in *Youth: A Narrative, and Two Other Stories* (1902), it quickly becomes clear that Marlow has grown older, and changed. He has become far more reflective and troubled than his youthful counterpart in the earlier story, and these mid-life changes in Marlow have taken place before he sets off for Africa.

It also becomes clear that Marlow finds it more difficult to tell this second story. Only after what might be described as a "comedy of false starts", where long pauses and silences punctuate his broodingly uncertain remarks about Roman and British imperialism, does Marlow finally seem ready to begin. Even then, he begins uncertainly, with a distressing vagueness, describing his experience as "pitiful – not extraordinary in any way – not very clear either. No, not very clear. And yet it seemed to throw a kind of light." Marlow's journey can be seen as an inversion of Dante's journey from Hell to Paradise – which is how T.S. Eliot saw it in his poem "The Hollow Men" (1925). And if we are retracing Marlow's journey as something that started, like Dante's, in a kind of mid-life crisis, it is important to see how Marlow's "world of straightforward facts" and "surface-truths", as he describes them, has already begun to unravel before he sets foot in Africa, and even before he leaves Europe.

Like Conrad in 1890, Marlow crosses the Channel to sign his three-year contract to work as a fresh-water sailor in the Belgian Congo. Belgium and Brussels are never named, and Marlow always refers to Brussels as the "sepuchral city" – as T.S. Eliot refers to London as the "unreal city" in "The Waste Land" (1922).

In Brussels, Marlow's sense of the "unreal" or "absurd" is already pressing in when he sees the two secretaries "knitting black wool". They seem "uncanny or fateful", like the classical Parcae or

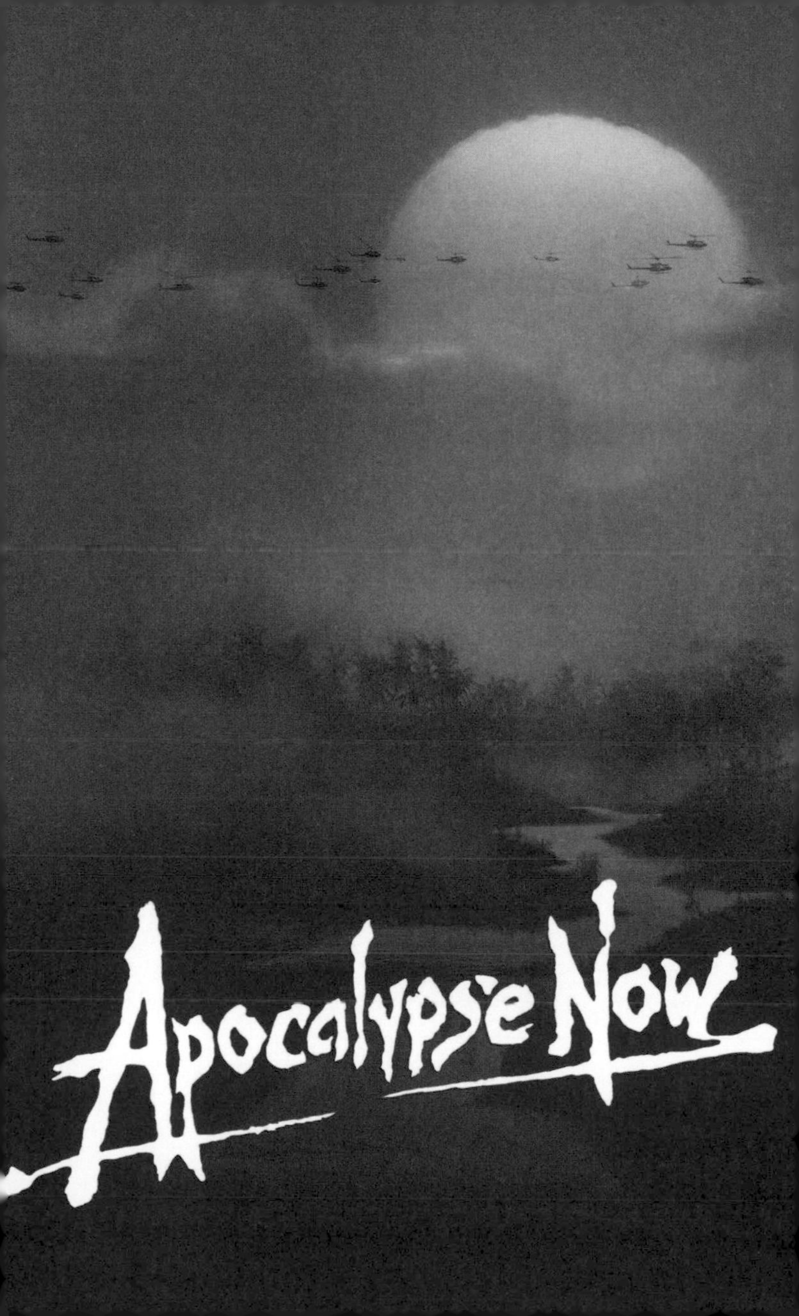
Apocalypse Now

the three Norns in Norse myth and Wagner's *The Ring*, who knit men's fates. Marlow says that he "often" recalled these two women when he was in Africa – confronting his "destiny" and all too probable death:

> *Often far away there I thought of these two, guarding the door of Darkness, knitting black wool as for a warm pall... Old knitter of black wool... Not many of those she looked at ever saw her again – not half, by a long way....*

The same macabre, dislocatingly surreal humour runs through Marlow's account of his meetings with the Company Director and the doctor who examines him. While waiting to meet the Director Marlow examines a "shiny" map of Africa in which different regions were marked in different colours – "all the colours of a rainbow" – that showed what Britain and various other countries had so far achieved in the "scramble for Africa":

> *There was a vast amount of red – good to see at any time, because one knows that some real work is done in there...*

Marlow, however, is "going into the yellow" – the million or so square miles that King Leopold II of Belgium had secured "to run an over-sea empire, and make no end of coin by trade". And there, in

the middle, is the Congo: "Dead in the centre",
and "fascinating – deadly – like a snake. Ough!"

While Marlow is lost in these thoughts a door
opens and "a skinny forefinger beckoned me into
the sanctuary":

*Its light was dim, and a heavy writing desk
squatted in the middle. From behind that
structure came out an impression of pale
plumpness in a frock-coat. The great man
himself. He was five feet six, I should judge,
and had his grip on the handle-end of ever
so many millions.*

After "about forty-five seconds", when he signed
"some document" promising "not to divulge any
trade secrets", Marlow "found" himself back in the
waiting room". Marlow the narrator recalls: "It
was just as though I had been let into some
conspiracy – I don't know – something not quite
right; and I was glad to get out." Even more
disconcerting is the meeting with the old company
doctor who checks his pulse ("Good, good for
there") and then "with a certain eagerness asked
me whether I would let him measure my head":

*'I always ask leave, in the interests of science, to
measure the crania of those going out there,' he
said. 'And when they come back too?' I asked.
'Oh, I never see them,' he remarked; 'and,*

*moreover, the changes take place inside, you
know.' He smiled, as if at some quiet joke.*

Later, when Marlow has left Europe but still
before he has set foot in Africa, his sense of the
absurd becomes more acute. While Marlow is
travelling down the coast, he watches a French
warship firing missiles into the jungle:

*In the empty immensity of earth, sky, and
water, there she was, incomprehensible, firing
into a continent. Pop, would go one of the six-inch
guns; a small flame would dart and vanish, a
little white smoke would disappear,
a tiny projectile would give a feeble screech – and
nothing happened. Nothing could happen. There
was a touch of insanity in the proceeding...*

When his ship delivers mail to the warship Marlow
learns from a French seaman that "the men in that
lonely ship were dying of fever at the rate of three a
day". As for the invisible natives who were the
target of this "incomprehensible" but constant
assault, they are called "enemies".

While still journeying down the African coast
and passing "places with farcical names, where the
merry dance of death and trade goes on", Marlow
sees the coast itself as an "enigma" that every day
"looked the same, as though we had not moved".
At least, he reflects, the "voice of the surf" was a

"positive pleasure": "something natural that had its reason, that had a meaning". "Now and then", when "a boat from the shore appeared", "paddled by black fellows", that "gave one a momentary contact with reality":

They wanted no excuse for being there. They were a great comfort to look at. For a time I would feel I belonged still to a world of straight-forward facts; but the feeling would not last long. Something would always turn up to scare it away. The general sense of vague and oppressive wonder grew upon me.

When Marlow finally arrives at the Company's Outer Station, he finds "a scene of inhabited devastation". Some of the inhabitants are not alive or even dead, like "a boiler wallowing in the grass" or "an undersized railway-truck lying there on its back with its wheels in the air". When he hears a "slight clinking" behind him, Marlow turns to see half a dozen Congolese natives in a chain gang:

Black rags were wound round their loins, and the short ends waggled to and fro like tails. I could see every rib, the joints of their limbs were like knots in a rope; each had an iron collar on his neck, and all were connected together with a chain whose bights swung between them, rhythmically clinking.

These natives are not "enemies"; they are "called criminals" and are being punished, according to "the outraged law" that has "come to them", "like the bursting shells, as an insoluble mystery from the sea". The terrible shock of seeing the chain gang becomes worse when Marlow sees the native guard who follows this gang of "criminals". When the guard sees Marlow he "hoists his weapon to his shoulder"; but he "was speedily reassured, and with a large, white, rascally grin, and a glance at his charge, seemed to take me into partnership in his exalted trust". Marlow is

NIGGERS

'Nigger', descended from the Latin 'niger', meaning black. As early as 1619 John Rolfe describes African slaves shipped to Virginia as 'negars'. The term was common in the late 19th century, used by Conrad (*The Nigger of the Narcissus,* 1897) but also Dickens and Mark Twain. In his autobiographic *Life on the Mississippi* (1883), Twain reports usage of the term, though he himself uses the term 'negro'. The 215 occurrences of the word in *Adventures of Huckleberry Finn* (1885) have proved a continuing source of controversy; a 2010 edition removed the references. In *A Dictionary of Modern English Usage* (1926), H.W.Fowler states that applying the word to "others than full or partial negroes" is "felt as an insult by the person described, & betrays in the speaker, if not deliberate insolence, at least a very arrogant inhumanity". By the 1900s, the term had become perjorative, a change reflected in the title of the indeed a partner: "After all. I also was a part of the great cause of these high and just proceedings." When he watched the French gunship firing on a continent, and registered that absurdity, his shock carried his sense that what was being done was not only absurd but murderous: the invisible natives who "needed no excuse for being there" were doubtless being killed or maimed. But seeing the chain gang and then seeing its guard's "reassured" smile is far worse, because that smile of "partnership" forces Marlow to recognise his own complicity. He has indeed become part of

---

National Association for the Advancement of Coloured People, founded in 1909. Over the course of the 20th-century 'coloured' has given way to 'black', and subsequently 'African American'.

The term became unequivocally offensive later in Britain, where even in the 1950s mainstream uses such as the Nigger Boy, a brand of sweet, the Mississipi canning company Negro Heat, Nigger Head Tobacco, and the colour 'nigger brown' persisted in common usage. In response to his wife's declaration, in 1969, that 'woman is the nigger of the world', John Lennon produced the song "Woman is the Nigger of the World", about the universal exploitation of woman, a decision that the American Civil Rights lobby found extremely inflammatory, but Lennon is not the only figure to have adopted the term as referring to the oppressed – the leader of the Front de Libération du Québec called his 1968 autobiography *White Niggers of America*. Agatha Christie's *Ten Little Niggers,* published in 1939, continued to appear under the title until it was re-named, in the early 1980s, *And Then There Were None.* ◆

this "noble cause". It is then not enough to plead that he is just doing his job.

The "appalled" Marlow makes for some trees he has seen, "to stroll in the shade for a moment". He then finds himself within a "grove of death" that resembles a scene from Dante's *Inferno*:

Black shapes crouched, lay, sat between the trees leaning against the trunks, clinging to the earth, having coming out, half effaced within the dim light, in all the attitudes of pain, abandonment, and despair.

As the "horror-struck" Marlow reflects, these dying natives were "not enemies, they were not criminals, they were nothing earthly now, – nothing but black shadows of disease and starvation, lying confusedly in the greenish gloom":

Brought from all the recesses of the coast in all the legality of time contracts, lost in uncongenial surroundings, fed on unfamiliar food, they sickened, became inefficient, and were then allowed to crawl away and rest.

Of course Marlow's suggestion that these natives are "helpers" who are now being "allowed" to "rest" is blisteringly ironic. They are "dying slowly – it was very clear". Marlow's reference to "the legality of time contracts" is no less blisteringly ironic. Such contracts were a prevalent method of forcing uncomprehending natives into a fixed, often fatal term of slavery after some tribal head had been bribed with bits of copper wire or trinkets. For the doomed natives such "contracts" were "incomprehensible", another "insoluble mystery from the sea"; for Marlow, the contracts' "legality" is absurd because it is another vile pretext in the history of "masquerading philanthropy".

Although these "African" passages present the suffering of the natives as all too real, and appalling, the same passages also seem unreal or surreal, like vivid hallucinations or (to borrow Marlow's phrase) "hints for nightmares". They show the effect of what was being done to the natives, while also showing the effect this has on Marlow.

The natives' world has already been shattered, in the interests of the "noble cause" that boils down to "imbecile rapacity". Marlow's own "world of straightforward facts", in what we like to call the *real* world, is now unravelling more quickly. He is increasingly "appalled", not only by the actualities of what is being done in this "merry dance of death and trade" but by his own complicity, and by the all too familiar justifications of what is being done – that is, by the ideology of imperialism, the talk of "legality", of "mutual benefit" and "the White Man's burden", or, before setting out, his own "excellent" aunt's all too representative chatter about "weaning those ignorant millions from their horrid ways".

By this stage in Part One of *Heart of Darkness* all such imperialist ideology has become unreal and absurd to Marlow; being British and believing in "work" and "efficiency" can no longer help him to keep some "hold on the world of redeeming facts". That world is falling apart, and the three parts of *Heart of Darkness* mark different stages in its disintegration.

What makes Marlow come to put his faith in Kurtz?

Few critics have troubled to ask themselves why *Heart of Darkness* is divided into three parts, though Conrad's structure – and it is of course Conrad's, not Marlow's, or the primary narrator's – is important and deliberate.

The tripartite structure of *Heart of Darkness* can be seen as an inversion of Dante's *The Divine Comedy.* In Dante's case the structure was imposed on him from outside, as it were, since his journey takes him from Hell, through Purgatory, and into Paradise. In an ironic echo, the three parts of *Heart of Darkness* reflect different stages in Marlow's trip to Africa and in his mental deterioration.

The first part shows how he gradually loses his

grasp of the everyday world, starts to wonder about his sanity and, finally, comes to believe in Kurtz. As we have seen, Marlow's "world of straightforward facts" has begun to unravel even before he sets off for Africa, and perhaps even before he crosses the Channel to sign his three-year contract in the "sepulchral" city, but his increasing sense of unreality doesn't become acute until he finally arrives at the Company's Outer Station and sees the chain gang, and the dying natives in the grove of death that recall Dante's *Inferno*.

But this African Inferno is man-made, and a foreign import. The very way in which the chain gang's guard smiles, when he feels "reassured" that Marlow is part of the "noble cause" – or, to borrow a key phrase in Lord Jim, "one of us" – drives home Marlow's sense that he is now complicit.

At this stage of Part One, Marlow is still at the Outer Station. He has to wait ten days – "an eternity" – before he can set off with "a caravan of sixty men, for a two-hundred mile tramp" on foot to the Central Station, through a country where "the population has cleared out a long time ago", leaving only "abandoned villages" and the "pathetically childish" "ruins of grass walls":

Day after day, with the stamp and shuffle of sixty pairs of bare feet behind me, each pair under a 60-lb. load. Camp, cook, sleep, strike camp,

*march. Now and then a carrier dead in harness,
at rest in the long grass, with an empty water-
gourd and his long staff lying by his side. A great
silence around and above. Perhaps on some
quiet night the tremor of far-off drums, sinking,
swelling, a tremor vast, faint; a sound weird,
appealing, suggestive, and wild – and perhaps
with as profound a meaning as the sound of bells
in a Christian country.*

Since the only other white man with Marlow is
"rather too fleshy" he keeps fainting and then gets
"fever, and had to be carried in a hammock slung
under a pole". When Marlow finally arrives at the
Central Station and meets, and loathes, the
Company Manager, he discovers that the steamer
he was to command has been wrecked, two days
before his arrival. As we later learn, the wrecking
of the steamer is almost certainly part of a plot on
the part of the Manager and his underlings to kill
the Company's most successful ivory trader, Kurtz,
by depriving him of vital supplies. At this point in
his story, however, Marlow the narrator merely
hints, without explaining, that this alleged accident
was more suspicious than Marlow the protagonist
supposed at the time:

*I did not see the real significance of that wreck at
once. I fancy I see it now, but I am not sure – not
at all.*

There is another such hint in Marlow's first meeting with the Company Manager, who guesses that it will take "some months" to repair the wreck, in order for Marlow to make the journey to the Inner Station where the situation was "grave, very grave" since Mr. Kurtz was "ill". The Manager then seems to pluck a precise estimate from nowhere: "let us say three months before we can make a start. Yes. That ought to do the affair." The enraged Marlow "flung out of his hut", convinced that the man "was a chattering idiot". But "Afterwards I took it back when it was borne in upon me startlingly with what extreme nicety he had estimated the time requisite for the 'affair'."

At the beginning of Part Two – some 18 pages later for the reader, but three months later for Marlow – he overhears enough of a conversation between the general manager and his uncle to understand that the manager has deliberately planned to leave Kurtz in the Inner Station without supplies for "nine months". This revelation is a good example of what has been called "delayed decoding" – the way in which the reader, like the protagonist, only later learns the significance of something which has been said or done.

So now, for the first time, Marlow the protagonist and the reader can understand that there has been a conspiracy to kill Kurtz. This of course provides the likeliest explanation of the wreck of the steamboat—though not quite certain:

years later, Marlow the narrator is still "not sure" – just two days before he arrived at the Central Station, after his punishing 200 mile trek. But this isn't clear in Part One.

At the end of Part One, Marlow is full of doubts about the Company he is serving, though he has no evidence of foul play. While trying, not very successfully, to suppress these doubts, he eagerly sets to work repairing the steamer so he can head up-river to find Kurtz:

> *In that way only it seemed to me I could keep my hold on the redeeming facts of life Still, one must look about sometimes, and I saw this station, these men.*

But his work cannot be completed without rivets "to stop the hole", and there are no rivets in the Central Station. Marlow had seen rivets lying all over the ground in the Outer Station, so he knows there are plenty available. But they don't come. By the end of Part One, Marlow has been stuck in the Central Station for three frustrating months, just as the Company Manager predicted (or planned) and has almost abandoned his concern with "work" and "efficiency".

The final paragraph of Part One shows in a subtle way how two different responses to this unbearable situation have now become curiously mingled:

I had given up worrying about the rivets. One's capacity for that kind of folly is more limited than you would suppose. I said Hang! – and let things slide. I had plenty of time for meditation, and now and then I would give some thought to Kurtz. I wasn't very interested in him. No. Still, I was curious to see whether this man, who had come out equipped with moral ideas of some sort, would climb to the top after all, and how he would set about his work when there.

On the one hand Marlow knows and says that "work" is his best way of keeping "a hold on the redeeming facts of life". In his essay "Well Done", Conrad writes: "For the great mass of mankind the only saving grace that is needed is steady fidelity to what is nearest to hand and heart in the short moment of each human effort." True, but sometimes, a man must ask questions. What is his "efficiency" serving? What if the job turns out to be acting as a guard in a concentration camp? That question isn't confronted in Conrad's essay, but it is in *Heart of Darkness*, and it has become ever more pressing for Marlow the protagonist when he faces "this station, these men" and when, at the end of Part One, he says "Hang!" and lets "things slide".

On the other hand Marlow has by now heard a great deal from "these men" about the mysterious but apparently idealistic Kurtz, whom they evidently hate, fear and envy. By this time Marlow has also realised that the men he loathes suspect him of being part of what he calls Kurtz's "gang of virtue", the benevolent liberal reformers who believed they could bring educational and spiritual enlightenment to the dark places of the earth. It is not surprising that, as Marlow lets "things slide" and seems dangerously near to collapse, he gives "some thought to Kurtz", as the one man whose example might help him to hold himself together. He says that he "wasn't very interested in him", but also admits to being "curious" about "this man, who had come out equipped with moral ideas of some sort". Marlow is ready to make the old mistake of supposing that his enemies' enemy must be his friend.

How does Marlow learn the truth about Kurtz?

When Part Two begins and Marlow learns of the plot to kill Kurtz, there is a sense in which he (and the first-time reader) can at last understand what has been happening; but there is another, more subtle sense in which he is trapped by his own wishful thinking about a man he does not know.

As he journeys up-river, Marlow's need to believe in the man he is seeking is paramount. For example, he never wonders how Kurtz could send so much "prime" ivory when he has nothing to trade with, since his Inner Station was "by that time bare of goods and stores". When he overhears the manager's account of how Kurtz had decided to return to his "lonely and deserted station", Marlow fancied that he "seemed to see Kurtz for the first time"; "I did not know the motive. Perhaps he was just simply a fine fellow who stuck to his work for its own sake."

Nothing could be more wrong, but once he has embarked on the long journey up-river, his sense of purpose revives: he is sustained not by any desire to serve the atrocious Company but by his wish to rescue – and listen to – Kurtz. The journey up-river becomes a race against time in two ways. He wants to rescue and save Kurtz, but he also needs Kurtz to save or rescue him from his utterly disillusioned view of what he calls "the dust-bin of progress" and "the dead cats of civilization". Simply doing his job, or being British, is now not enough.

This need is not something that Marlow consciously recognises until the steamer is a few miles from Kurtz's Inner Station and the natives attack it. Only then, when Marlow's cannibal helmsman has been killed and Marlow supposes that Kurtz himself must be dead, does he discover how much he has come to need Kurtz: "I made the strange discovery that I had never imagined him as doing, you know, but as discoursing." When he confesses to his listeners on the Nellie how "I couldn't have felt more of a lonely desolation somehow, had I been robbed of a belief or had missed my destiny in life", one of his listeners sighs and mutters "Absurd!" Marlow then launches into his most angrily exasperated tirade against these Pillars of Society: "This is the worst of trying to tell... Absurd be – exploded!"

If we are considering the journey as part of an action story, the natives' attack is the climax of Part Two, and by the end of it Marlow has still not seen Kurtz – who matters so much not because of what he is, but because of the way he has come to matter for Marlow the protagonist. But the real climax of Part Two comes in its final pages, after the attack. Marlow the protagonist is reeling from his belief that Kurtz is dead and that he will now never meet or hear him; Marlow the narrator turns on his old friends for their inability to "understand" why this matters so much, and becomes so excited that the chronology of events – and his narrative – goes haywire.

When he tries to resume his story he talks about "voices" and the "girl" and the "lie" for reasons that neither Marlow's friends nor first-time readers are in a position to understand – another example of delayed decoding. But what we do begin to learn, as his narrative becomes more coherent again, is the degree of Kurtz's wickedness.

Instead of ending with some final "Dr Livingstone, I presume" meeting, Part Two ends with Marlow's stunningly unexpected encounter with one of Kurtz's followers, the Russian 'harlequin" or "man in patches". The "harlequin" is brave, sympathetic, but quite mad in his hero-worship of Kurtz who, he says, "enlarged my mind": in other words, he is a parody of what Marlow himself might have become if he had been intoxicated by the "discoursing" he had so longed to hear, insisting that

> *"You can't judge Mr Kurtz as an ordinary man. No, no no! Now – just to give you an idea – I don't mind telling you, he wanted to shoot me, too, one day – but I don't judge him."*

The harlequin, says Valentine Cunningham in his book *In The Reading Gaol*, looks like someone who has "wandered in from a Dostoevsky novel". With his brightly coloured patches – "blue, red, and yellow" – he is "a living emblem of Africa's dividedness, a walking, talking version of the map that Marlow encountered in Brussels". This "mobile sculpture of Africanness" seems so unreal that he becomes, in Cunningham's words, "a key focus of Marlow's rhetoric of defeated conception and harassed narration". His very existence, says Marlow, was improbable, inexplicable, and altogether bewildering. He was an insoluble problem. It was inconceivable how he had existed.

The harlequin's nationality is clearly significant: hatred of Russians ran deep in

Conrad's Polish blood.* The terror at the heart of "this fiction's darkness", writes Cunningham,

> is like an archetypal Polish nightmare, concocted by a man with a German name and a Russian friend, harsh reminders of the two enemies traditionally given to squeezing Poland in their unfriendly pincer embrace.

The Russian harlequin illustrates the breadth of international involvement in Africa's exploitation and vividly reinforces Marlow's sense of complicity with the whole imperial enterprise.

The affinities between the two are plain. There is the old book which Marlow finds in a "heap of rubbish" in the bush: *An Inquiry into Some Points of Seamanship.* This reassuring volume, radiating the values of the British Merchant Navy, and with its "honest concern for the right way of going to work", turns out, ironically, to belong to the harlequin. The connection between the two is rubbed in further by the harlequin's claim of their shared brotherhood of the sea, his acceptance of Marlow's tobacco and his cadging from Marlow a pair of his old shoes. The gift of the shoes seals the connection – from henceforth the Russian will walk in Marlow's shoes. He becomes like Marlow's doppelganger, or

* "Il y aura des Russes. Impossible!" Conrad replied to Cunninghame Graham's invitation to sit on an international peace-meeting platform.

mirror-self, a Mr Hyde to Marlow's respectable Dr Jekyll. The harlequin even begs a few cartridges for his Martini-Henry rifle, going off with his copy of the seamanship manual in one pocket (dark blue), while another bulges with cartridges. This second pocket is bright red, an ironic reminder of Marlow's remark about the red on the Brussels map – "so much of the real work [is] done in there". As Cunningham says, the complicity of Marlow and the British Empire he represents with Kurtz and his sidekick "could not have been made clearer".

But Marlow is not the harlequin, and by the time he finally meets Kurtz in Part Three he is aware what a monster Kurtz is. He has already recalled his stunned first sight of the human heads on poles around Kurtz's hut – the remains of men Kurtz has had killed. We have heard, too of Kurtz's chilling report for the Society for the Suppression of Savage Customs. Marlow's attitude to the eloquence of this, as he reads it, recalls the French poet Verlaine's famous explosion, "Take eloquence and wring its neck!" He notes sardonically the "burningly noble words" and "the magic current of phrases" – and then the shocking "scrawled" postscript: "Exterminate the brutes!" Neither the report nor its terrible postscript represent what Kurtz believes, since he believes in nothing. Hollow to the core, he is no more than a highly gifted bundle of voracious appetites. In Dostoevsky's *The*

Brothers Karamazov, Ivan famously maintains that if God is dead everything is permitted, and that applies well enough to Kurtz, who feels nothing to restrain him from gratifying his various lusts.

Faced with what he learns of Kurtz, Marlow is not even "prepared to affirm" that Kurtz's life was "worth the life we lost in getting to him": in other words, the life of this half-English, half-French "genius" was not, in Marlow's view, worth more than that of the cannibal helmsman who is killed as they approach the Central Station.

Kurtz, as Ian Watt has argued, "dramatizes Conrad's fear of the ultimate directions of 19th century western thought" and its justifications for imperialism and naked commercialism. "All Europe," Marlow tells us, "had contributed to the making of Kurtz", and Kurtz's motives, and his fate are deeply representative. He represents the Victorian idea of progress, the idea of the "survival of the fittest" and of the superiority of the white man, and he embodies the view of destiny which Sartre summed up in his definition of man as "the being whose plan it is to become God".

Never just crudely mercenary, Kurtz goes out to Africa as a member of "the gang of virtue". He is "an emissary", says the brickmaker Marlow meets in the Outer Station, "of pity, and science, and devil knows what else". He is a poet and a painter, too, and a man of words. But he becomes a monster: the jungle, says Marlow, "whispered to him things about himself which he did not know, things of which he had no conception till he took counsel with this great solitude". At home, says Watt, everything had conspired "to keep Kurtz in ignorance of his true self; the police stopped him from devouring others or being devoured; but in the solitude his 'forgotten and brutal instincts' revealed themselves as potent forces in his biological inheritance..."

This is what Marlow discovers in Part Two of *Heart of Darkness*.

As he puts it himself, he has peeped down the abyss into which Kurtz stared; he has been retracing Kurtz's journey, is stirred when he sees Kurtz's African mistress, and will finally meet Kurtz's fiancée, described as "the Intended" in the climax of Part Three. But although the Marlow of Part Three maintains his characteristic concern with conduct – his sense that there are things that must be done and things that must never be done – his discovery of what Kurtz has become casts him back on his own "inner strength", and he finds it is no longer enough.

When Kurtz dies and is buried in a "muddy hole", Marlow has his massive, nearly fatal breakdown.

Cartoon from an 1899 edition of Life magazine entitiled 'The White (?) Man's Burden,' showing caricatures that represent the United States and three European countries (from front, United Kingdom, Germany, and France) as they are carried on the shoulders of shoulders of non-Caucasian men

TEN FACTS
ABOUT *HEART OF DARKNESS*

1.

Works inspired by *Heart of Darkness* include T.S. Eliot's *The Waste Land*, and Francis Ford Coppola's *Apocalypse Now*, set in Vietnam and Cambodia, in which Marlon Brando played Kurtz. The only film adaptation of *Heart of Darkness* itself was in 1993, with John Malkovich starring as Kurtz.

5.

Of Conrad's 20 volumes of work produced over three decades, 37 of Conrad's short stories, novellas and novels appeared first in serial form.

6.

T.S. Eliot appended a quotation from *Heart Of Darkness* – "Mistah Kurtz, he dead" to the original manuscript of his poem *"The Hollow Men"*. The title may originate from Kurtz, referred to as a "hollow sham" and "hollow at the core".

7.

The explorer Henry Morton Stanley has been cited as a possible influence for the character of *Kurtz*. Stanley was supposedly infamous for his violence against his porters during his time in Africa. Conrad may also have taken details from the *Life of Georges Antoine Klein*, an agent who died aboard Conrad's steamer and was interred along the Congo, much like Kurtz. Conrad may also have encountered Leon Rom, who became chief of the Stanley Falls Station. In 1895 a British traveller reported that Rom had decorated his flower bed with the skulls of 21 victims, including women and children.

2.

Conrad was introduced to English at an early age, when his father was translating the works of Shakespeare, Dickens and Victor Hugo in order to support the household; his English remained heavily accented for the rest of his life, and was his third language, after Polish and French. He became a British subject in 1886, when he changed his name from Józef Korzeniowski to Joseph Conrad.

3.

Conrad, who came from an aristocratic Polish family, declined the knighthood offered by Ramsay MacDonald in 1924. (He is said initially to have mistaken it for an income tax demand.). Conrad is in good literary company — Thomas Hardy, Rudyard Kipling and John Galsworthy also refused the honour.

4.

Despite being an atheist throughout most of his life, Conrad accepted last rites and was buried as a Roman Catholic.

2.

Conrad was introduced to English at an early age, when his father was translating the works of Shakespeare, Dickens and Victor Hugo in order to support the household; his English remained heavily accented for the rest of his life, and was his third language, after Polish and French. He became a British subject in 1886, when he changed his name from Józef Korzeniowski to Joseph Conrad.

3.

Conrad, who came from an aristocratic Polish family, declined the knighthood offered by Ramsay MacDonald in 1924. (He is said initially to have mistaken it for an income tax demand.). Conrad is in good literary company — Thomas Hardy, Rudyard Kipling and John Galsworthy also refused the honour.

4.

Despite being an atheist throughout most of his life, Conrad accepted last rites and was buried as a Roman Catholic.

5.

Of Conrad's 20 volumes of work produced over three decades, 37 of Conrad's short stories, novellas and novels appeared first in serial form.

6.

T.S. Eliot appended a quotation from *Heart Of Darkness* – "Mistah Kurtz, he dead" to the original manuscript of his poem *"The Hollow Men"*. The title may originate from Kurtz, referred to as a "hollow sham" and "hollow at the core".

7.

The explorer Henry Morton Stanley has been cited as a possible influence for the character of *Kurtz*. Stanley was supposedly infamous for his violence against his porters during his time in Africa. Conrad may also have taken details from the *Life of Georges Antoine Klein*, an agent who died aboard Conrad's steamer and was interred along the Congo, much like Kurtz. Conrad may also have encountered Leon Rom, who became chief of the Stanley Falls Station. In 1895 a British traveller reported that Rom had decorated his flower bed with the skulls of 21 victims, including women and children.

8.
Since 1963 the preferred text of the novella has been Robert Kimbrough's collation of four of the story's significant forms: the 1899 serial version, the manuscript, the typescript, and the final, revised form published in 1902.

9.
Other famous works published in 1902 include Beatrix Potter's *The Tale of Peter Rabbit* and Kipling's *Just So Stories*. In 1899, the year of the serialisation of *Heart of Darkness* in Blackwood's Magazine, Helen Bannerman's *Little Black Sambo* appeared, selling more than a million copies before being withdrawn in 1988.

10.
Conrad had various run-ins with the law. Having joined the French Merchant Navy at the age of 16, he became involved in gun-running along the Spanish coast in 1877-78 for the Carlist cause, an episode fictionalised in *The Arrow of Gold* (1919). The gun-running ship was scuttled to avoid capture, and in 1878, after a bout of gambling, Conrad attempted suicide by shooting himself in the chest with a revolver.

How does Marlow think of the jungle?

The first chapter of Leonard Woolf's absorbing novel *The Village in the Jungle* (1913) tells us that "All jungles are evil, but no jungle is more evil than that which lay about the village of Beddagama". Woolf very daringly tells his story from the native point of view. Long before he wrote his novel, and even before Conrad finished *Heart of Darkness* in 1899, a growing number of novels and stories had shown white expats coming apart in the tropics and learning too late that the jungle is evil. *Heart of Darkness* is part of that tradition, but it also subverts it.

"To Marlow... the jungle seems like an enormous threatening quasi-human personage," writes the American critic J. Hillis Miller. On the contrary, the jungle in *Heart of Darkness* is no more like a "quasi-human personage" than the Marabar Caves in E.M. Forster's *Passage to India*. Conrad's story deconstructs the conventional idea of the white man degenerating when he encounters evil in the jungle: the evil is rather something the white man brings to the jungle, and visits on natives who "wanted no excuse for being there". Conrad shows, like Robert Louis Stevenson in "The Beach of Falesá", how the white men were usually dreadful specimens, and anything but "emissaries of progress" – they were, as Conrad put it in one of his letters to Cunninghame Graham, "souteneurs, sous-offs, maquereaux, fruits–secs" [pimps, non-coms, bullies, and failures of all sorts].

Marlow shows his disgust with the white men he meets; indeed, in one of the central ironies of the story, he supposes that his enemies' enemy – Kurtz, the worst exploiter of them all, whom these dreadful specimens all fear or hate – must be his friend. However, in so far as Marlow thinks of the jungle, he thinks of it not as evil but as violated. Only after being in Africa for months, and only when he has embarked on the thousand-mile journey up the Congo to find Kurtz, does Marlow begin to think of the jungle – or rather, its "stillness" – as something threatening or "vengeful". If we read more attentively – attending to verb tenses as well as the crucial distinction between Marlow the narrator and Marlow the protagonist – we can see how Marlow the protagonist's attitude to the jungle changes and develops over some months, and many hundreds of miles. The day after his first meeting with the general manager at the Central Station, Marlow reflects (and the verb tense confirms that this was the protagonist's reflection, not the narrator's):

And outside, the silent wilderness surrounding this cleared speck on the earth struck me as

something great and invincible, like evil or truth,
waiting patiently for the passing away of this
fantastic invasion.

"Like evil or truth": at this stage, the "invincible"
but violated wilderness "struck" Marlow as
something "waiting patiently", not as something
unambiguously "threatening". The ambiguity
persists a few pages later: when Marlow is talking
with the bricklayer, he wonders whether the jungle's
"stillness" is "meant as an appeal or as a menace":

All this was great, expectant, mute, while the
man jabbered about himself. I wondered
whether the stillness on the face of the immensity
looking at us two were meant as an appeal or
as a menace.

The first reference to "the hidden evil" and the
"profound darkness" of the jungle's "heart" comes,
significantly, not in Part One but early in Part Two –
only seven pages later for the reader, but three
months later for Marlow the protagonist – and
does not come from Marlow. It comes at the
crucial moment when he and the reader learn for
the first time that the general manager has in effect
been trying to murder Kurtz, of whose success and
fame he is jealous. The manager's uncle warmly
approves of the plan to kill Kurtz by cutting off the
supplies he needs, to live as well as "trade", and

Marlow then hears the vile uncle telling his vile nephew to "trust" the jungle:

"Ah! My boy, trust to this – I say, trust to this." I saw him extend his short flipper of an arm for a gesture that took in the forest, the creek, the mud, the river, – seemed to beckon with a dishonouring flourish before the sunlit face of the land a treacherous appeal to the lurking death, to the hidden evil, to the profound darkness of its heart.

In this last sentence one word after another – "seemed", "dishonouring", "treacherous" – confirms that the uncle's view of the jungle's "hidden evil" is not to be ascribed to Marlow himself, and the very next sentence makes this comically clear:

It was so startling that I leaped to my feet and looked back at the edge of the forest, as though I had expected an answer of some sort to that black display of confidence.

Marlow then determines to "help" Kurtz if he can. Of course Kurtz may already be dead, and the thousand-mile journey to Kurtz's Inner Station will take another "two months". Once he has embarked on the dangerous journey up-river, Marlow no longer feels that the jungle is "patiently waiting" for an end to the "fantastic invasion" or violation. Instead, Marlow reflects that "this stillness of life did not in the least resemble a peace":

It was the stillness of an implacable force brooding over an inscrutable intention. It looked at you with a vengeful aspect.

The sentence that so offended F.R. Leavis actually marks a new and critical stage in Marlow's sense of the extremity of his situation. His earlier, strange idea of the "stillness" as something "meant" is developing. The jungle now seems "threatening", to use Miller's word — or as the unnerved Marlow puts it, "implacable" and "vengeful".

However, this corrective analysis is still insufficient, because the word "it", in the sentences just quoted, does not refer to the jungle. The antecedent for this "it" is the "stillness" in the jungle, not the jungle itself. The narrating Marlow goes on to claim that the "mysterious stillness" that was "watching me", or Marlow the protagonist, "at my monkey tricks", now "watches you fellows performing on your respective tight-ropes for — what is it? half-a-crown a tumble".

In other words, Marlow the protagonist's sense of the "stillness" in question has changed, or developed. First it was the "patient" stillness of the "silent wilderness surrounding us". Then Marlow sees it as "the stillness on the face of the immensity looking at us"; this facial "stillness" is still ambiguous, but is more disturbing because it seems to express something "meant" that Marlow cannot make out or decipher. And then the "stillness of life" seems, to Marlow, like "the stillness of an implacable force", although its meaning and "intention" are "inscrutable".

What is happening here is complicated in something like the way that Thomas Hardy's extraordinary late poems about his dead wife are complicated. In the many years that they were both alive, Hardy and his wife found it difficult to live together, let alone love each other. But these strange, late or too late love poems recall different moments and events with an almost unbearably moving sense of what might have been: the poems interweave past and present, passionately recalling moments in the past that might have led to a different present and future, by shaping correspondingly different earlier and later selves. T. S. Eliot's uncharacteristic and deeply moving poem "La Figlia che Piange" similarly shows how the speaker's memories of moments that "compelled my imagination" are both informed and transformed by his imaginative sense of what might have been but is now forever lost.

At this crucial point in *Heart of Darkness*, the shifts in tense show how the narrating Marlow is recalling, recapturing and to that extent both reliving and re interpreting Marlow the protagonist's earlier, terrifying experience of feeling "cut off for ever from everything you had known once – somewhere – far away – in another existence perhaps". As he continues his journey up-river, there are times when he is too busy to attend to the "it" which threatens him: "I did not see it any more; I had no time." His attention is fully caught up with guiding the steamboat through the channel.

> When you have to attend to things of that sort, to the mere incidents of the surface, the reality – the reality, I tell you – fades. The inner truth is hidden – luckily, luckily. But I felt it all the same...

So what is this "it", which Marlow keeps referring to and which, in this extraordinary passage, is suddenly associated with some "inner truth" that is opposed to fading "surface" realities? And the "it" whose "mysterious stillness" Marlow feels was "watching me at my monkey tricks", is – as Marlow the narrator suddenly and aggressively insists – the same "it" that "watches you fellows performing". The "fellows" on the yawl Nellie are clearly not being watched or menaced by the African jungle. So what is "it"?

So what is "it"?

When John Ruskin coined the term "pathetic fallacy" he was warning his readers of the dangers in ascribing human features or emotions to non-human objects or creatures. He took as one of his examples Coleridge's lines,

> The one red leaf, the last of the clan,
> That dances as often as dance it can...

Literary and poetic examples of the "pathetic fallacy" are frequently pretty and sentimental in that way – but Conrad's aren't: they are highly conscious and usually alarming or sharply ironic.

So when we are told in *Nostromo* (1904) that the huge mountain Higuerota's "cool purity seemed to hold itself aloof from a hot earth" we might reflect that a mountain cannot be "pure" and cannot "hold itself aloof". But the paragraph goes on to describe a political "riot" that is going on under the mountain and is observed from a distance:

> *Horsemen galloped towards each other, wheeled round together, separated at speed. Giorgio saw one fall, rider and horse disappearing as if they had galloped into a chasm, and the movements of the animated scene were like the passages of a violent game played upon the plain by dwarfs*

mounted and on foot, yelling with tiny throats,
under the mountain that seemed a colossal
embodiment of silence.

To see the "riot" in this way, as if through the wrong end of a telescope, is inevitably belittling, as is the old Italian revolutionary Giorgio's vigilant but contemptuous point of view of the "animated scene" and its participating "dwarfs". Higuerota's "colossal embodiment of silence" then seems to pass its own contemptuous comment on human littleness and insignificance.

The use of the "pathetic fallacy" is deliberately ironic and anything but pretty. It illustrates Conrad's view of the menacing indifference or hostility of the natural world towards human life. What Higuerota's "colossal embodiment of silence" embodies, that might well seem alarming from a human point of view, is the absence of any connection between the non-human world and the human world. That is what he means by "it" in *Heart of Darkness*.

In his first great novel, *The Nigger of the 'Narcissus'* (1897), the unreflective and heroic Singleton braves the terrible affliction of a storm, saving the ship and its crew, and then falls into an exhausted sleep. When he wakes, the old man, who "had never given a thought to his mortal self", arrives at the devastating moment of

Opposite: Conrad aboard a ship

"completed wisdom" that makes him feel
that he has been "broken at last":

*He had to take up at once the burden of all his
existence, and found it almost too heavy for his
strength. Old! He moved his arms, shook his
head, felt his limbs. Getting old... and then? He
looked upon the immortal sea with the awakened
and groping perception of its heartless might; he
saw it unchanged, black and foaming under the
eternal scrutiny of the stars; he heard its
impatient voice calling for him out of a pitiless
vastness full of unrest, of turmoil, and of terror.
He looked afar upon it, and he saw an immensity
tormented and blind, moaning and furious, that
claimed all the days of his tenacious life, and,
when life was over, would claim the worn-out
body of its slave.*

The "it" that Singleton sees and hears, when he
wakes and looks upon the sea again with an
"awakened and groping perception of its heartless
might" is being personified as though "it" were like
something human: "it" seems "tormented and
blind, moaning and furious", with a "voice" that
can call for and claim the now "broken" Singleton.
But of course this "it" is not like anything human.
Instead, what the "it" refers to is terrifyingly real
because it is everything that there is out there, in
the non-human world, and terrifying because it is

so devastatingly indifferent to human endeavours and the world of human values.

The seemingly vengeful "it" that Marlow the protagonist feels menaced by on his journey upriver, as well as the "it" that Marlow the narrator so surprisingly says is "watching" his old friends on the *Nellie*, is in one obvious respect unlike the "it" that Singleton gropingly perceives: the moaning, violent sea is utterly different to the jungle's mysterious stillness. Yet there is a far more important similarity between these different "its".

Unlike Singleton, Marlow is intensely reflective. While still journeying down the African coast he had felt a "general sense of vague and oppressive wonder" that "grew upon me". This "wonder" increases and becomes more oppressive on his thousand-mile journey upriver, penetrating "deeper and deeper into the heart of darkness". He feels "cut off for ever from everything you had known once – somewhere – far away – in another existence perhaps".

The new "realities of this strange world" seem "overwhelming" to Marlow, while the practical things he must constantly "attend to" in doing his job seem to belong to "the mere incidents of the surface" or "surface-truth". To be sure, the constant work keeps him going in a literal as well as metaphorical sense: his situation is in that respect less dangerous than it was at the end of Part One, when he "said Hang! – and let things slide". Indeed, his old respect for work had movingly revived when he was still some "fifty miles below the Inner Station" and discovered a book in a hut, *An Enquiry into some Points of Seamanship*:

> *Not a very enthralling book, but at the first glance you could see there a singleness of intention, an honest concern for the right way of going to work, which made these humble pages, thought out so many years ago, luminous with another than a professional light. The simple old sailor, with his talk of chains and purchases, made me forget the jungle and the pilgrims in a delicious sense of having come upon something unmistakably real.*

Yet the "facts of life" that this book recalls are not enough to sustain Marlow for long as he journeys upriver. Nor are the "surface-truths" enough to stave off his obscure sense of some other "inner truth", that is usually and "luckily" hidden, pressing in from without.

In Marlow's case, as in Singleton's, it doesn't seem helpful to say, like Hillis Miller, that the "it" seems to Marlow like some "quasi-human personage", and it seems actively misleading to refer, like Miller, to Marlow's "belief" in darkness as a "metaphysical principle". Marlow is no more inclined than Singleton to metaphysics or religion. The "it" that Marlow talks about might be better described as a concrete absence, or lack: a lack, because it is an absence; concrete because, as in the case of the unreflective, heroic Singleton, the absence is something real that is out there in the non-human world, and provides no support whatever for the human world or autonomous human values.

One way of trying to understand what Marlow means by "it" is to consider the philosopher Arthur Schopenhauer's famous distinction between the "World as Will" and the "World as Representation" (i.e. what we *want* to believe about the world and what the world is *actually like*). The younger Conrad was greatly influenced by Schopenhauer's pessimistic views, and it would certainly be possible to argue that Singleton's "groping" sense of "a pitiless vastness" grew out of this distinction, as did Marlow's increasingly menaced sense of a contrast between "surface-facts" and some "inner truth".

This way of explaining the "it", however, would have been lost on Marlow himself, who, as we have noted, is unbookish, with no taste for Continental metaphysics. (We learn in *Lord Jim* how he even gave up on reading the Scottish historian and essayist, Thomas Carlyle.) Although the Marlow of *Heart of Darkness* and *Lord Jim* is more inwardly troubled than the Marlow of "Youth", he is also pragmatic in a very English way. Like his Polish creator, he is profoundly concerned with how to live

– with a code of conduct, or what anthropologists call an *ethos*. He is – to use a very English concept that Marlow himself uses in *Lord Jim* – incorrigibly *decent,* and despite the existential crises that trouble him so deeply he never surrenders his concern to live decently. It is this tension between his own sense of decency and his overpowering sense of a menacing "it" in the world outside him which makes his story so poignant.

To take an important example: in the dangerous journey up the Congo he is both puzzled and impressed by his cannibal helmsman's "restraint". And when his helmsman is killed Marlow does not hesitate to pronounce that his helmsman's life was worth far "more" than that of Kurtz, the "hollow sham" who lost all sense of "restraint". Marlow's very strong concern with conduct – his sense that there are things you just must do and things that you just must not do, like abandoning your ship and its passengers in Lord Jim's case, or, in Kurtz's case, taking part in murderous rituals – involves an ethos that he feels he must live by even if it conflicts with the values of those around him, or with the vast, indifferent "it" which makes a mockery of any code of conduct.

In his book, *Islam Observed*, the anthropologist Clifford Geertz explores the relationship between our *ethos* – the way we do things, "and like to see things done" – and our *mythos*, or world view, the "collection of notions" we have "of how reality is at base put together". Geertz then argues that the "heart" of the religious perspective, or way of looking at the world, is not the theory that beyond the visible world lies an invisible one, and not the religious doctrine that some divine presence broods over this world, but "the conviction that the values one holds are grounded in the structure of reality, that between the way one ought to live and the way things really are there is an unbreakable inner connection". The *mythos*, or world view, and the *ethos* are mutually confirming.

In Conrad there is no corresponding conviction that "the values one holds are grounded in the inherent structure of reality", and no "unbreakable inner connection" of the kind that Geertz locates at the heart of the religious perspective. Indeed, Conrad constantly accentuates the *rift* between *mythos* and *ethos*, or between "seeing from inside", in Geertz's sense, and "seeing from outside", in a more helplessly or aggressively sceptical fashion.

In *Heart of Darkness*, the confused, alarmed Marlow comes to doubt whether the values he holds are "grounded in the inherent structure of reality". This doubt, this awareness of a world indifferent to humanity and human values, is the "it" to which he frequently refers.

The same kind of metaphysical or existential doubt assails Marlow in *Lord Jim*:

For a moment I had a view of the world that

*seemed to wear a vast and dismal aspect of
disorder, while, in truth, thanks to our unwearied
efforts, it is as sunny an arrangement of small
conveniences as the mind of man can conceive.*

In both *Heart of Darkness* and Lord Jim, Marlow
feels he is being "robbed" of a "belief" – or of the
"few simple notions" that a man must "cling to" if
he wants "to live decently and would like to die
easy". What is breaking down in each case is
Marlow's own sense of any inner connection
between mythos and ethos.

In different ways, all Conrad's central
characters experience a similar feeling to the sense
of disjunction felt by Marlow in *Heart of Darkness*.
They are all shadowed by a similar force, by a
similar feeling of the hostility of the world, to the
feeling he describes as "It".

What does Kurtz mean by "The horror! The horror!"?

It is never more important to distinguish between
Marlow the narrator and Marlow the protagonist
than when considering Kurtz's famous last words:
"The horror! The horror!" We cannot know,
because Marlow does not and cannot know what
Kurtz meant by his last words, which may not even
have been his last words. Kurtz could have been

contemplating his own death, or the ruin of his insane ambitions, or the loss of his ivory, or the loss of either or both of his women. He could have been recognising and lamenting the impossibility of engaging in further "unspeakable rites". He might have been passing judgment on himself, or life, or the universe in general, or his last meal, or an internal pain. In J.M. Coetzee's novel *Foe* Susan Barton says of the unknowable Friday: "No matter what he is to himself, what he is to the world is what I make of him". It would greatly clear the air if Marlow could say something like that, but Marlow cannot think like that.

We can still ask, more sensibly, what Marlow makes of Kurtz's last words, or what they mean to Marlow; but the demonstrable and dismaying answer to that question is: different things at different times. His attitude to Kurtz is never a settled one, and not surprisingly critics are divided about the meaning of his last words. Trilling believes that Marlow continues to see Kurtz, even after his death, and despite his terrible crimes, as a "hero of the spirit".

Consider that Kurtz is a progressive and a liberal and that he is the highly respected representative of a society which would have us believe that it is benign, although in fact it is vicious. Consider too that he is a practitioner of several arts, a painter, a writer, a musician, and into the bargain a political orator. He is at once the most idealistic and the most practically successful of all the agents of the Belgian exploitation of the Congo. Everybody knows the truth about him which Marlow discovers – that Kurtz's success is the result of a terrible ascendancy he has gained over the natives of his distant station, an ascendancy which is derived from his presumed magical or divine powers, that he has exercised his rule with an extreme of cruelty, that he has given himself to unnameable acts of lust... It is to this devilish baseness that Kurtz yielded himself, and yet

---

CONRAD, HARDY AND PESSIMISM

Conrad, like Thomas Hardy, is famous for his pessimism. In both there is a strong element of anti-rational primitivism: "Where ignorance is bliss/'Tis folly to be wise." The narrator of Hardy's *The Return of the Native* laments that "thought is a disease of the flesh". In his "Author's Note' to *Victory*, Conrad remarks: "The habit of profound reflection... is the most pernicious of the habit formed by civilized man." What makes mankind tragic, he writes on another occasion, "is not that they are the victims of nature, it is that they are conscious of it".

Conrad was more cosmopolitan than Hardy and his pessimism has a different emphasis to Hardy's. While Hardy, as Cedric Watts says, "has a bitter sense of the ways in which destiny tortures the innocent and sensitive,

Marlow, although he does indeed treat him with hostile irony, does not find it possible to suppose that Kurtz is anything but a hero of the spirit.

Trilling finds the "famous deathbed cry" ambiguous, unsure whether Kurtz is referring to the approach of death or to "his experience of savage life", but sees the fact that Kurtz could utter this cry at the point of death, while Marlow himself, when death threatens him, "can know it only as a weary greyness, marks the difference between the ordinary man and a hero of the spirit".

Conrad has a more Augustan sense of the general vanity of human wishes". When Cunninghame Graham complained that Singleton in *The Nigger of the Narcissus* would have been a stronger character if he'd been educated, Conrad wrote back in exasperated tones wondering what kind of knowledge Singleton should have been educated into:

> ... do you mean the kind of knowledge which would enable him to scheme, and lie, and intrigue his way to the forefront of a crowd no better than himself? Would you seriously... cultivate in that unconscious man the power to think. Then he would become conscious – and much smaller – and very unhappy. Now he is simple and great like an elemental force... Would you seriously wish to tell such a man: 'Know thyself'. Understand that thou art nothing, less than a shadow, more insignificant than a drop of water in the ocean, more fleeting than the illusion of a dream. Would you? ◆

Is this not the essence of the modern belief about the nature of the artist, the man who goes down into that hell which is the historical beginning of the human soul, a beginning not outgrown but established in humanity as we know it now, preferring the reality of this hell to the bland lies of civilization that has overlaid it?

Valentine Cunningham makes a similar point:

Kurtz, the hollow man, the person intimately associated with the unspeakability of Africa, with the unspeakable rituals conducted there by both blacks and whites, the man whose very name is a lie*, is nonetheless a voice, a word-monger whose word not only persists but has a degree of affirmation that Marlow seeks and signally fails to achieve. Marlow has to be content with knowing life only as a "riddle"... Kurtz has the positive assurance of the believing damned, Marlow the lukewarm Laodiceanism [indifference to politics and religion] of the troubled agnostic.

In his modestly titled but immensely perceptive *A Preface to Conrad*, Cedric Watts discusses Kurtz's last words as an "interpretative crux". Marlow, says Watts, suggests four possible meanings for "The horror! The horror!":

"Kurtz (says Marlow) – Kurtz – that means short in German – don't it? Well, the name was as true as everything else in his life – and death. He looked at least seven feet long."

(1)   Kurtz condemns as horrible his corrupt
       actions, and this "judgment upon the
       adventures of his soul" is "an affirmation, a
       moral victory".

(2)   Kurtz deems hateful but also desirable the
       temptations to which he had succumbed: the
       whisper had "the strange commingling of
       desire and hate", and therefore is not a moral
       victory at all, it seems.

(3)   Kurtz deems horrible the inner nature of all
       humans: "no eloquence could have been so
       withering to one's belief in mankind as his
       final burst of insincerity", where his stare
       'penetrate[d] all the hearts in the darkness'.

(4)   Kurtz deemed horrible the whole universe:
       "that wide and immense stare embracing,
       condemning, loathing all the universe...
       'The horror!'"

Watts brilliantly identifies a difficulty that previous
critics had ignored, but his conclusion is less
convincing. He goes on to observe that the
"elements of contradiction" in Marlow's analyses
of Kurtz's words make him " rather glibly
hyperbolic and emotively portentous":

We may speculate whether Marlow is here the

mouthpiece of a Conrad who is under strain, or whether, on the contrary, a coolly lucid Conrad is deploying an over-insistent and confused Marlow.

What this analysis fails to take into account is what F.R. Leavis and other critics have failed to take into account: the difference between Marlow the protagonist and Marlow the narrator. What Marlow feels during the experience itself, and what he feels later, as he looks back on and reinterprets his experience, are very different, as is clear if we attend to the significant shifts in the narrative between past and present tenses.

Marlow the protagonist's initial response to Kurtz's last words was fascinated but interrogative and uncertain, as his reference to "some image" and "some vision" indicates:

> *I saw on that ivory face the expression of sombre pride, of ruthless power, of craven terror—of an intense and hopeless despair. Did he live his life again in every detail of desire, temptation, and surrender during that supreme moment of complete knowledge? He cried in a whisper at some image, at some vision – he cried out twice, a cry that was no more than a breath – "The horror! The horror!"*

Marlow goes off to eat his dinner, and when the manager's boy rushes in to report "Mistah Kurtz—

Scenes from Francis Ford Coppola's Apocalypse Now

he dead!" Marlow does not stir:

> *All the pilgrims rushed out to see. I remained,*
> *and went on with my dinner. I believe I was*
> *considered brutally callous. However, I did not*
> *eat much... I went no more near the remarkable*
> *man who had pronounced a judgment upon the*
> *adventures of his soul on the earth.*

That last sentence is more removed from the events and the protagonist's immediate responses; the narrator may already be pressing in, to prepare us for his later affirmative reinterpretation. The narrator is very much in evidence a moment later he says, "But of course I am aware" – not *I was aware* – "that next day the pilgrims buried something in a muddy hole." Then he adds a dramatic, single-sentence paragraph:

> *And then they very nearly buried me.*

Instead of explaining what happened to him, Marlow the narrator tells us, clearly and unequivocally, that this unexplained but nearly fatal event is "the reason why I affirm that Kurtz was a remarkable man": "He had something to say. He said it."

In all this there is no hint that Marlow had thought anything like this at the time, or detected any kind of "affirmation", or "moral victory" in

Kurtz's last words. But immediately after describing his first responses to the dying Kurtz, Marlow the narrator launches into a long, complicated paragraph that explains "the reason why" he now affirms that Kurtz's final "pronouncement" represented some kind of "moral victory".

In the following quotation the emphases are mine, and mark shifts into the present tense when Marlow the narrator presents his more affirmative interpretation of what Kurtz's final "pronouncement" meant. This Marlow confides that he has "wrestled with death":

I was within a hair's-breadth of the last opportunity for pronouncement, and I found with humiliation that probably I would have nothing to say. *This is the reason why I affirm that Kurtz was a remarkable man.* He had something to say. He said it. Since I had peeped over the edge myself, *I understand better the meaning of his stare*, that would not see the flame of the candle, but was wide enough to embrace the whole universe, piercing enough to penetrate all the hearts that beat in the darkness. He said it. He had summed up – he had judged. 'The horror!' He was a remarkable man. *After all*, this was the expression of some sort of belief; it had candour, it had conviction, it had a vibrating note of revolt in its whisper, it had the appalling face of a glimpsed truth – the strange commingling of desire and hate. *And it is not my own extremity I remember best – a vision of greyness without form filled with physical pain, and a careless contempt for the evanescence of all things, even of this pain itself. No! It is his extremity that I seem to have lived through.* True, he had made that last stride, he had stepped over the edge, while I had been permitted to draw back my hesitating foot. *And perhaps in this is the whole difference; perhaps all the wisdom, and all truth, and all sincerity, are just compressed into that inappreciable moment of time in which we step over the threshold of the invisible. Perhaps! I like to think my summing-up would not have been a word of careless contempt. Better his cry – much better. It was an affirmation, a moral victory paid for by innumerable defeats, by abominable terrors, by abominable satisfactions. But it was a victory! This is why I have remained loyal to Kurtz to the last, and even beyond, when a long time after I heard once more, not his own voice, but the echo of his magnificent eloquence thrown to me from a soul as translucently pure as a cliff of crystal.*

Marlow's earlier and later interpretations of Kurtz's words are both clearly interpretations, and they are no less clearly discrepant. Since Conrad has juxtaposed the conflicting interpretations, we

can see from the shifting tenses and points of view
how Marlow the narrator's own affirmation is
dramatized, and answers to his need to believe
that Kurtz was not as evil as he clearly was – or, at
least, that Kurtz has recognised and acknowledged
the evil he has done and somehow redeemed
himself by doing so. Here we might remember
Nietzsche's maxim: "Always doubt what you most
want to believe."

The final sentence in the quoted passage is
another matter, since neither the first-time reader
nor Marlow's immediate audience can understand
what he means by it. What was the "echo"? Whose
was the soul "as translucently pure as a cliff of
crystal"?

This is another instance of what will be delayed
decoding; we can't know the answers to these
questions until we have nearly finished a first
reading of *Heart of Darkness.* Only in the last
pages do we learn of Marlow's meeting with
Kurtz's "fiancée", or "Intended" – and of the lie he
tells her. If Conrad had presented the meeting
earlier we wouldn't have been so well able to
understand Marlow's tormented sense that he
must lie to her or, to put that differently, has no
right to afflict her with the truth. But because
Conrad makes this meeting the climax of his story,
we cannot understand the reference to her "soul"
in the quoted passage – or another, earlier
reference to her – on a first reading. Conrad

himself clearly understood the demands he was making on the reader. In a letter to his publisher William Blackwood he observes, speaking of his general method in writing stories: "I depend upon the reader looking back upon my story as a whole."

So what has happened to Marlow in between Kurtz's death and his re-evaluation of Kurtz's last words? The answer is that he has had a complete and nearly fatal breakdown, a breakdown from which he can only recover by hiding from himself the truth about Kurtz.

How significant is Marlow's breakdown?

Most critics attach little weight to Marlow's mental collapse, because it is only alluded to, but its severity can be measured by the fact that he can barely remember anything about his journey home, which would have taken many months. After the dramatic single-sentence paragraph – "And then they very nearly buried me" – there follows an immensely long paragraph which begins with something like Mark Twain's famously witty protest that reports of his death had been "exaggerated": "However, as you see," says Marlow,

I did not go to join Kurtz there and then. I did not. I remained to dream the nightmare out to the

end, and to show my loyalty to Kurtz once more.
Destiny. My destiny! Droll thing life is – that
mysterious arrangement of merciless logic for a
futile purpose.

After this long, laden, three-page, 31-sentence
paragraph – with its insistence that Kurtz's dying
"cry" was "an affirmation" – Marlow's narration
rushes on. In the next paragraph, which is also long
and complicated, he is somehow "back in the
sepulchral city" (Brussels). Like Conrad before
him, he hasn't been able to fulfil his three-year
contract: he has returned, or been returned, to
Europe after just a few months, as a nervous
wreck.

No, they did not bury me, though there is a period
of time which I remember mistily, with a
shuddering wonder, like a passage through some
inconceivable world that had no hope in it and no
desire.

More than 20 years before T.S. Eliot wrote "The
Waste Land" (1922), Marlow's responses to being
back in the "sepulchral city" sound like the
responses of the main speaker to the "unreal city"
(London) in Eliot's poem.

Unreal City,
Under the brown fog of a winter dawn,

The crowd flowed over London Bridge, so many,
I had not thought death had undone so many.
Sighs, short and infrequent, were exhaled,
And each man fixed his eyes before his feet.

Eliot's main speaker has evidently, like Eliot, suffered a massive breakdown, but he insists that the cause of this was not in himself but in some wider, cultural breakdown. The more reticent, deeply English Marlow never makes that kind of claim. Instead of arguing, in Eliot's evasively fragmented but didactic way, that his own massive and devastating breakdown had some general cultural cause, he chooses not to talk about it.

Still, Conrad's story provides two measures of just how devastating Marlow's breakdown was. The first, already mentioned, is that Marlow's return journey would have taken months. Conrad's own journey up the Congo to "the centre of Africa" took nearly five months. The journey back was quicker, as Marlow's would have been: "The brown current ran swiftly out of the heart of darkness, bearing us towards the sea with twice the speed of our upward progress." But it would still have taken two months for him to reach Leopoldville, and hammock bearers would then have had to carry him to Matadi.

The second measure of just how devastating Marlow's breakdown was comes in a sentence that many readers – and critics – glide through, without, perhaps, reflecting on how much it reveals. When Marlow first sees Kurtz's fiancée, described as "the Intended" – who is still "in mourning", and who comes "floating towards me in the dusk" – he recalls:

> *It was more than a year since his death, more than a year since the news came; she seemed as though she would remember and mourn for ever.*

In other words, it is now "more than a year" since the "pilgrims" buried Kurtz and then "nearly buried me". Yet Marlow is still in Brussels. We learn that he was being looked after by his "dear aunt", whose endeavours to "nurse up my strength seemed altogether beside the mark. It was not my strength that wanted nursing, it was my imagination that wanted soothing."

As Marlow puts it, in an almost breathtaking example of English understatement: "I dare say I was not very well at that time."

Wandering alone in Brussels, "resenting the sight of people hurrying through the streets", the still convalescent, desperately thin-skinned and neurotic Marlow has not yet turned into the enigmatic, contained Marlow we see in the story's opening pages, sitting "cross-legged" with "an ascetic aspect" and resembling "an idol".

The fact that Marlow the narrator is so reticent about discussing what was evidently a devastating and nearly fatal breakdown is dramatically revealing. Conrad's story presents the evidence for this – for something Marlow the narrator no less evidently doesn't want to discuss or confront – and his skill in doing so shows why *Heart of Darkness* is an early modernist classic that anticipates "The Waste Land" (1922).

We now know that Eliot had wanted to make "Mistah Kurtz he dead" the epigraph for *The Waste Land*, and that Ezra Pound discouraged this idea, saying that Conrad's story would not bear that kind of weight. So Eliot used the Conradian quotation as the epigraph for his next major poem, "The Hollow Men" (1925). Critics and commentators on that poem have agreed that Conrad and Dante are both major "sources" for "The Waste Land". Eliot sets his allusions to them against each other, as though they represented opposed alternatives – faith on the one hand, nihilism on the other. And while one can argue with Eliot's belief that Conrad was a nihilist, just as one can argue with his assumption that James Joyce's *Ulysses* represented an immense "panorama of futility", one can't doubt that Eliot was influenced by both Conrad and Joyce.

Eliot also understood the influence of Dante on Conrad, and seems to have been very alive to the ways in which Conrad's story recalls Dante.

Opposite: map of colonial Africa, circa 1902

Marlow's journey, as we have noted, is a grim parody of Dante's, and his meeting with Kurtz's fiancée – the Intended – at the end of his story, when he is still convalescing, is a grim parody-version of Dante's Beatrice. Beatrice represents, and believers might say that she *is*, the Holy Truth, whereas the Intended represents not Truth but a life dependent on an illusion – and arguably, though this is one of the most important questions Conrad raises in *Heart of Darkness*, an illusion that is not worth having.

Why does Marlow lie to the Intended?

In Human, All Too Human (1886), Nietzsche considers Dante's *La Divina Commedia* as the supreme instance of the way in which art can "divinely transfigure precisely those ideas which we now recognize as false", and "glorify humanity's religious and philosophical errors". He then goes on to reflect, with the painful self-division that is so marked throughout *Human, All Too Human*, that the greatest artistic achievements had depended upon "belief in the absolute truth" of what we now regard as errors or illusions. Nietzsche famously declares that "We have art in order not to perish of the truth", while insisting that the truth, for modern man, can no longer sustain such "divine transfigurations".

In the first two parts of Dante's *Divine Comedy* Dante's guide, who leads him through Hell and then through Purgatory, is the great Roman poet Virgil; but then, as a Roman pagan, Virgil cannot lead Dante through Paradise. His new guide appears, or reappears: it is Beatrice, the girl Dante had adored in his youth and then, after her early death, went on idolising throughout his adult life. But Beatrice has been divinely transfigured, so that she now appears as the embodiment of Holy Truth or as the Church itself. Dante is overcome, and cannot meet her eyes.

Critics have often discussed the allusions to Dante's *Inferno* in the "grove of death" episode in *Heart of Darkness*, where Marlow strolls "into the shade" and finds he had "stepped into the gloomy circle of some Inferno" peopled by black shapes "in all the attitudes of pain, abandonment and despair". They don't suggest that Conrad is once again recalling Dante when Marlow finally meets Kurtz's "Intended", but it is worth noting how she appears as a parody-Beatrice "in mourning", whose "faith" is an illusion and whose "halo" is "ashy", a trick of the light:

She had a mature capacity for fidelity, for belief, for suffering. The room seemed to have grown darker, as if all the sad light of the cloudy evening had taken refuge on her forehead. This

fair hair, this pale visage, this pure brow, seemed
surrounded by an ashy halo from which the dark
eyes looked out at me.

Looking into these eyes is painful, because their
glance "was guileless, profound, confident, and
trustful", and because her faith in Kurtz and his
ideals – her "belief" that "his goodness shone in
every act" – is an illusion.

But, after being "in mourning" for "more than a
year", she talks on and on, about "the loss to me –
to us!", about Kurtz's "promise", his "greatness",
"his generous mind", while Marlow reflects that
"she talked as thirsty men drink", "easing her pain
in the certitude of my sympathy". After praising
Kurtz as a great man, she says, or cries: "But you
have heard him! You know!" Marlow's ironic but
deeply troubled response produces what may be
the most laden sentence Conrad ever wrote:

Yes, I know, I said with something like despair in
my heart, but bowing my head before the faith
that was in her, before that great and saving
illusion that shone with an unearthly glow in the
darkness, in the triumphant darkness from which
I could not have saved her – from which I could
not even defend myself.

Of course Marlow does not and cannot share
the girl's faith. He sees it and describes it as an

illusion, as something that is not true. Even when he says that her faith "shone with an unearthly glow in the darkness", he is saying, quite unequivocally and very significantly, that it is not the "unearthly glow" but the "darkness" that is "triumphant" – something "from which I could not have saved her – from which I could not even defend myself".

He describes himself as feeling "something like despair in my heart, but" – and what a laden "but" this is! – "bowing my head before the faith that was in her, before that great and saving illusion..." That recalls and helps to explain his strange reference – many pages earlier, when he was beginning his tale, but much later in his actual life – to the need for a redeeming idea: "not a sentimental pretense but an idea; and an unselfish belief in the idea – something you can set up, and bow down before, and offer a sacrifice to..."

The idea of a "saving" or "sustaining" illusion also recalls Nietzsche, although Conrad certainly hadn't read any Nietzsche when he wrote *Heart of Darkness*, and perhaps never did. When considering any belief, Nietzsche's habit was to ask two questions. Of course the first was, is this true? But Nietzsche understood that some illusions are more important than others and usually went on to ask, what would a life be like that was lived according to this belief? Most of the great literature that we read is rooted in beliefs that we no longer share; but, as Martha Nussbaum has argued, one of the most important reasons for studying literature and "one very important link between philosophy and literature" is that literature helps us to "imagine vividly what a life would be like with and without" some particular belief, or illusion. And as both Nietzsche and Conrad realised, some illusions are necessary for survival itself.

Rightly or wrongly, Marlow is convinced that telling the Intended the truth would not only shatter her illusion but destroy the basis of her existence. (If he did tell the truth, after all, it couldn't just be about Kurtz's last words; he would also have to explain how wrong she was to believe that Kurtz's "goodness shone through every act".)

So when the Intended tells Marlow he must "know" about Kurtz's greatness, and Marlow says, "Yes, I know", he is equivocating or engaging – with increasing distaste, irritation and even "despair" – in a kind of double talk. Throughout this climactic meeting, which could be described as an undivine comedy, he allows and even encourages the Intended to suppose that he is being straight in his replies when he isn't.

"You knew him well," she starts – taking but not opening the packet of letters he has finally delivered. "Intimacy grows quickly out there," he replies, before offering a more Jesuitical equivocation: "I knew him as well as it is possible for one man to know another." That works well enough, but when she then says, "And you admired him", Marlow replies, more "unsteadily": "He was a remarkable man." The "appealing fixity of her gaze" forces him to add, "It was impossible not to -----", and she finishes his sentence for him, supplying the wished for but self-deluding words Marlow cannot:

> *"Love him," she finished eagerly, silencing me into an appalled dumbness. "How true! how true!"*

The sad comedy moves in a more dangerous direction when the girl insists that "His words, at least, have not died":

> *"His words will remain,"'I said.*
> *"And his example," she whispered to herself.*
> *"Men looked up to him, – his goodness shone in every act. His example –"*
> *"True" I said; 'his example too. Yes, his example. I forgot that."*

In her innocently remorseless fashion the girl replies, "But I do not. I cannot..." Marlow's ordeal intensifies when "She put out her arms as if after a retreating figure" – reminding him with the gesture of the African mistress who still haunts his imagination, and had seemed so much less

anaemically civilized than the sexless Intended.
The girl then unwittingly goes on pressing on
another dangerously tender nerve.

> She said suddenly very low, "He died as he lived."
>   "His end," said I, with dull anger stirring in me,
> "was in every way worthy of his life."
>   "And I was not with him," she murmured. My
> anger subsided before a feeling of infinite pity.
>   "Everything that could be done – "I mumbled.

We can almost hear Marlow's mumble turn into a
gulp, once he sees that he has now exposed himself
to the question that so inevitably follows:

> "You were with him – to the last?"
> "To the very end," I said shakily. "I heard his very
> last words...." I stopped in a fright.
> "Repeat them," she said in a heart-broken tone. "I
> want – I want – something – something – to – to
> live with."

When she persists in demanding "His last word—
to live with" Marlow braces himself, as if for some
dreadful duty:

> I pulled myself together and spoke slowly. "The
> last word he pronounced was—your name."
>   I heard a light sigh and then my heart stood
> still, stopped by an exulting and terrible cry, by

the cry of inconceivable triumph and of
unspeakable pain. "I knew it – -I was sure!"...
She knew. She was sure.

What caps this undivine, all too human comedy is
that we never discover and Marlow himself
appears not to know what the girl's real name is.
Hence the old joke, that the girl's real name is "The
Horror".

Critics divide about Marlow's lie. Robert Penn
Warren admires it and compares it to other
"charitable" lies in Conrad – "white" lies, told to
spare someone else's feelings rather than to
advance one's own interests. Others believe that
the Intended's illusion was not one worth
preserving – that she should have been made
aware of Kurtz's evil and that to spare her was
patronising and sexist.

And how charitable was the lie anyway? Did
Marlow perhaps tell it for his own benefit as much
as for the Intended's? Conrad leaves this open, but
it is interesting that it takes Marlow so long to visit
the Intended and return the packet of Kurtz's
letters. It has been "more than a year" since Kurtz
died, and Marlow has been convalescing in
Brussels for much or most of that time. He has
also become curious – in, we might guess, an
emotionally hungry or lonely way. As Marlow the
narrator reports, the convalescent protagonist has
written to the Intended, after studying "the girl's

portrait": "She struck me as beautiful – I mean she had a beautiful expression." Hmm. Having peeped into the abyss down which Kurtz stared, Marlow, who is still single in *Lord Jim* and the much later novel *Chance* (1915), is wanting to follow yet another of Kurtz's paths.

Given all this, it is surely unlikely that Marlow would want to tell the Intended a truth that so nearly destroyed the basis of his own existence. He has still not recovered after "more than a year". Since he so desperately wants to recover and rejoin the ranks and return to England – even if England can now never be more than a land of lost content – what right can he possibly have to afflict the "girl" with a devastating truth from which he himself is trying to escape, or recover?

The question becomes even more pertinent when one considers Marlow's attitude to women – not to women like Kurtz's African mistress, but to women who belong to what Ian Watt calls the "well-to-do and leisured class", like Marlow's aunt and the Intended. When, early in the story, Marlow finds it hard to convince his aunt that the Trading Company he is going to work for is run for profit, he comments: "It's queer how out of touch with truth women are. They live in a world of their own." Similarly, when he first talks of the Intended, he says: "Oh she is out of it – completely. They – the women I mean – are out of it – should be out of it. We must help them stay in that beautiful world of their own, lest ours gets worse."

Since Marlow believes that it is only through work that anyone can really learn the truth about life, Kurtz's Intended, says Watt, is in effect excluded from discovering reality.

It is by no choice of hers, therefore, that the Intended inhabits an unreal world; but because she does Marlow at the end finds himself forced to lie to her about Kurtz. One reason is that if he told the truth she would not have the necessary grounds in her own experience to be able to understand it; another is that since for all his seeking Marlow himself has found no faith which will move mountains, his nostalgia inclines him to cherish the faith that ignores them.

In a sense, of course, Marlow is trapped into saying what he does. Like so many lies, charitable or not, his lie to the Intended is triggered by a series of evasions from which, once the process has started, he cannot easily extricate himself. At first he doesn't lie, in a legalistic or literal sense. He engages, very awkwardly in a kind of double talk. The dramatic effect of this all-too-human "comedy" depends on the way Marlow the narrator recalls how Marlow the protagonist swung between discomfort and irritation as he delivered his equivocating replies.

That the question of why and whether he should have lied to the Intended deeply troubled Marlow the protagonist, and still troubles him when he narrates the story, is very clear. He writes, in the past tense, of his belief, after telling the lie, how it "seemed to me" – that is, to Marlow the protagonist,

> *that the house would collapse before I could escape, that the heavens would fall upon my head. But nothing happened...*

before adding, in the present tense (i.e. with his narrator's perspective):

> *The heavens do not fall for such a trifle.*

This sardonic remark, which seems sharply at odds with Marlow's earlier outburst about his hatred of lying, is symptomatic of the confusion he feels – a confusion which may have had something to with his decision to tell his friends on the Nellie about his experience, though this can never be more than speculation. Nonetheless Marlow's narrative concludes with these sentences:

> *The heavens do not fall for such a trifle. Would they have fallen, I wonder, if I had rendered Kurtz that justice which was his due? Hadn't he said he wanted only justice? But I couldn't. I could not tell her. It would have been too dark – too dark altogether...*

What is so distinctive about Conrad's view of the world?

It is strange that the author of *A Passage to India* should have complained that "we needn't try to write [Conrad] down philosophically, because there is, in this direction, nothing to write". The crisis that E.M.Forster inflicts on Mrs Moore in the Marabar caves is not unlike the crises that Conrad inflicts on Marlow, first in *Heart of Darkness* and then in *Lord Jim*. After her terrifying experience in the cave Mrs Moore feels that its annihilating boum-boum echo "began to undermine her hold on life by seeming to tell her: 'Pathos, piety, courage – they exist, but are identical, and so is filth. Everything exists, nothing has value.' Later, "suddenly, at the edge of her mind, Religion appeared, poor little talkative Christianity, and she knew that all its divine words from 'Let there be Light' to 'It is finished' only amounted to 'boum'."

In Part One of *Heart of Darkness*, Marlow speaks of work as the best or only way in which "I could keep my hold on the redeeming facts of life". But later, when he is journeying upriver, Marlow is increasingly disturbed by the jungle and his growing sense of the contrast between "surface" realities and some devastating "inner reality". He feels as though he has been "robbed of a belief".

And in *Lord Jim*, Marlow comes to feel that Jim's case – the extent to which Jim is "one of us" – calls into question his – Marlow's – own beliefs, even his seaman's sense of "the solidity of our craft":

> *"I was aggrieved against him, as though he had cheated me – me! – of a splendid opportunity to keep up the illusion of my beginnings, as though he had robbed our common life of the last spark of its glamour."*

In each of these cases, what the character comes to "know" is experienced as a frightening loss that threatens or "undermines" their "hold on life".

FIN DE SIÈCLE

In its broadest sense, the expression fin de siècle (literally 'end of century') refers to a kind of decadence, even degeneration, and the apocalyptic sense of the end of a phase of civilisation. The term is most closely associated with the artistic climate at the turn of the 19th century, encompassing the movements that reached their peak in the 1890s – Symbolism, Decadence and Aestheticism, most notably exemplified by artists such as Mallarmé, Toulouse-Lautrec and Debussy in Paris and Beardsley, Charles Conder and Oscar Wilde in England.

The ideas and concerns – the consciousness, in fact, of the fin de siècle – influenced the decades to follow, playing an important role in the birth of modernism. The expression tends to refer not to the change itself – which many people would

Given the similarity of Mrs Moore's experience in *Passage to India*, it is silly of E.M. Forster to disparage Conrad in the way he does. It may be, as Ian Watt argues in *Heart of Darkness and Nineteenth-Century Thought*, that Conrad is not philosophical in the way George Eliot and Thomas Hardy are: " we don't feel in the presence of logical arguments or moral lessons". But he is without doubt one of the more thoughtful of novelists, and a more profoundly modern one in his way of seeing the world, and writing about it, than Forster was.

He was in many ways a product of his time, and of his own, disjointed, pan-European upbringing and early life. He was widely read, not least in

date, in this instance, to the First World War – but rather the sense of its coming.

The pessimism which afflicted both Conrad and Thomas Hardy, and poets like Matthew Arnold and T.S. Eliot stemmed in part from the decline of religious belief and a general scepticism fuelled by scientists, philosophers and evolutionists like Darwin.

In 1898, the year most of *Heart of Darkness* was written, Conrad wrote again to Cunninghame Graham, with theatrically exaggerated despair. Like Hardy and H.G. Wells, he had been impressed and shaken by Lord Kelvin's second law of thermodynamics, which demonstrated that the universe was running down and that the sun would burn itself out:

> Of course reason is hateful – but why? Because it demonstrates (to those who have the courage) that we, living, are out of life – utterly out of it. The mysteries of the universe made of drops

science, and strongly affected by the late Victorian physicists who thought the planet was merely an accident resulting from the cooling gases of the sun and that the world would eventually come to a very cold end when the sun burnt itself out. As Watt argues, this dispiriting historical and scientific view pervades *Heart of Darkness*. Marlow's first remark, as the sun sets over London is: "And this also... has been one of the dark places of the earth" – and he harks back to the darkness which faced the first Roman settlers in Britain. Civilization, he, and his story, suggest, is merely a brief interruption in the darkness so that, in Marlow's words, "We live in the

of fire and clods of mud do not concern us in the least. The fate of humanity condemned ultimately to perish from cold is not worth troubling about. If you take it to heart it becomes an unendurable tragedy. If you believe in improvement you must weep, for the attained perfection must end in cold, darkness and silence.

The novels and poems of the period are full of a sense of loss, and the sense of morality being no more than a matter of convention is very strong in Conrad. The ardour for reform, virtue, knowledge, and even beauty, he told Cunninghame Graham in a letter, "is only a vain sticking up for appearances as though one were anxious about the cut of one's clothes in a community of blind men. Life knows us not and we do not know life – we don't even know our own thoughts." The world is "like a forest in which nobody knows the way. Faith is a myth and beliefs shift like mists on the shore." ◆

flicker". In the last sentence of *Heart of Darkness*, the primary narrator reflects, in a remark which shows how he himself has been affected by the story and reminds us that despite Marlow's attempt to cheat the darkness by lying, any such attempt is ultimately doomed:

The offing was barred by a black bank of clouds, and the tranquil waterway leading to the uttermost ends of the earth flowed sombre under an overcast sky – seemed to lead into the heart of an immense darkness.

Heart of Darkness is in tune with the apocalyptic note struck by other novelists of the 1890s and early 1900s, not just Hardy (see p.86) but the likes of H.G. Wells and Oscar Wilde in his *Picture of Dorian Gray*, where Lord Henry murmurs "*Fin de siècle*" and his hostess answers: "*Fin du globe*". As we have noted, Conrad shared Freud's gloomy sense that man is not a rational creature, and believed, like Freud, that the destructive tendencies of human beings must be controlled. He had no time for Christianity – "Christianity," he wrote in 1916, "is the only religion which, with its impossible standards has brought an infinity of anguish to innumerable souls on this earth" – and believed, as Watt puts it, that the "cardinal lesson" of experience is a full realization of our fragile, lonely and humble status in the natural order; and here any theoretical system, whether philosophical, scientific or religious, is likely to foster dangerous delusions of independence and omnipotence.

All of this is clear in *Heart of Darkness*, the clearest, shortest distillation of Conrad's world view. But clear too, through Marlow, is Conrad's belief in standards – in the notions of Duty, Restraint and Work which Marlow himself lives by and which, at first at least, keep him sane. A concern with conduct runs through all Conrad's work. In *Heart of Darkness* there is no doubt about his fiercely disapproving attitude to the activities of Leopold II's rapacious agents in the Belgian Congo, just as we never doubt, when we are reading *Nostromo*, that Conrad disapproves of the contemporary activities of the "Yankee Conquistadores" in Panama, and never doubt, when we are reading *The Secret Agent*, that he was horrified by the historical anarchist attempt to blow up the Greenwich Observatory in 1894.

In these and many similar cases, Conrad's correspondence confirms what is already apparent in the fiction. Yet when we try to "unpack" such specific seemingly firm judgements in the fiction, we find that they don't rest on any correspondingly firm moral or ideological sanctions. Rather, the fiction exposes such judgments and attitudes to a fiercely sceptical energy.

Nowhere is this sceptical energy more apparent

People gathered in the forest, at the passage of the steamboat captained by Conrad, the Roi des Belges, *Sankuru, 1888*

Belgian river station on the Congo River, 1889

than in what is widely considered his greatest work, *Nostromo*. The crisis which afflicts the journalist, Decoud, abandoned and alone on a deserted island, is a more extreme version of the crisis which afflicts Marlow in *Heart of Darkness*. Decoud commits suicide, and the presentation of his final days is so powerful that we have no difficulty in understanding that he kills himself when he comes to doubt "his own individuality" and "the reality of his action", seeing life as "a succession of senseless images"; his fate, we are told, illustrates the need for "the sustaining illusion of an independent existence as against the whole scheme of things of which we form a helpless part".

Even more unnervingly, in *Under Western Eyes*, we see the activist Razumov brought to such "a state of peculiar irresolution" that while he wonders whether he should "continue to live", he is unable even to contemplate, like Decoud, something as positive as actually killing himself:

> The idea of laying violent hands upon his body did not occur to Razumov. The unrelated organism bearing that label, walking, breathing, wearing these clothes, was of no importance to anyone, unless maybe to the landlady.

The fates suffered by Decoud and Razumov are extreme versions of what Marlow goes through.

Both experience, in their different ways, the sense of isolation and disconnectedness that the narrator of *Heart of Darkness* experiences in the jungle, but while Marlow is shattered by what happens to him, and has a nervous breakdown, they are broken for ever. Both books, like *Heart of Darkness*, portray the universe as a hard, remorseless machine; both see the individual as, in Cedric Watts's words, "a solitary consciousness amid a mirage-like flux".

Conrad once told Cunninghame Graham: "Sometimes I lose all sense of reality in a kind of nightmare effect produced by existence." "All is illusion," he wrote to Edward Garnett, a friend and senior reader at his publishers, and he liked to quote Calderon's words, "*La vida es sueño*" ("Life is a dream"), which is recalled in Decoud's thought in Nostromo: "All this is life, must be life, since it is so much like a dream.". "We live, as we dream – alone," says Marlow in *Heart of Darkness*.

As Ian Watt says, Conrad's narrators, especially Marlow and the narrator of Nostromo, have the "cynical" habit of applying the term "illusions" to ideals, thoughts, observations and feelings – even love is termed merely "the strongest of illusions" in *Nostromo*. At the same time Conrad strongly believed that it was impossible to live without some illusions. He would have agreed with Ibsen's Dr Relling, in *The Wild Duck*: "If you take away the *life lie* from the average man, you take his happiness as well."

In Conrad's world, as in Nietzsche's, language is just another way in which people hide from reality and deceive themselves, and the problems Marlow encounters in telling his story in *Heart of Darkness* reflect his, and Conrad's sense of the difficulties in the way of any real understanding between people, of the way people delude themselves with words, and of the inadequacy of language to deal with reality. "Conrad, like T.S. Eliot, was occupied with frontiers of consciousness beyond which words fail, though meaning itself still exists," writes D.C.R.A. Goonetilleke.

Our "prime experience" of *Heart of Darkness*, as readers, says Valentine Cunningham, is the awful collapse of Marlow's "rhetorical confidence". The story is first and foremost "an experience of the failure of language". The concern with words and how little they tell us is evident throughout, from Marlow's narrative hesitancies to the indecipherable scrawl on the seamanship manual (which turns out to be Russian) and the way in which what Marlow calls Kurtz's "noble words" are undercut by the dreadful postscript: "Exterminate the brutes!" So Marlow himself, the would-be truth-teller, succumbs, in the end, to lies, despite telling us lies are tainted and associated in his mind with death.

Yet the failure of language is intimately linked with the experience which generates it. The collapse in confidence in the values of white imperialism which Marlow comes to feel is responsible, in Cunningham's words, "for generating this famous display of narrative and rhetorical powerlessness, this decline in story-teller's confidence". One leads inevitably to the other:

> As with all of modernism's exemplary engagements with despair – its devoted revulsion from narrative, detective-style success – the rhetorical... narrative issues never arise in *vacuo*. There is always, whether for Browning or James, for Joyce or Conrad, some experience or sense of moral, theological, political, social loss that is also significantly, and I would argue fundamentally, in play.

Heart of Darkness, as Cunningham says, is "unpicking a tradition of the English novel in which writing and colonizing have gone intimately together". Robinson Crusoe, the founding father of the modern novel, was a man "with a pen in one hand and a gun in the other. The Russian with cartridges in one pocket and a book in the other, Kurtz the ivory trading poet, are Crusoe's updated analogues." Gone are the moral certainties of Defoe, the assumption that western nations had a "God-given right to plunder and enslave".

Yet while Conrad was pessimistic, was he, as critics like Brantlinger and Edward Said argue, nihilistic? Here, perhaps, it is worth drawing a distinction between what one might call radical scepticism, which can turn on itself, and terminal scepticism, or nihilism. Conrad is presenting a frightening, godless world in which, to borrow a phrase Marlow uses in Lord Jim, there is no "sovereign authority", and our ideas of what we know or think we know are constructs, with no ultimate sanctions or support system.

This, many would say, amounts to nihilism. But Conrad the novelist was not nihilistic: in his works, the very meaninglessness of institutions and values made the question of how to live all the more pressingly urgent. His response to the infernal machine and the "remorseless process" is also fiercely constructive, like a builder all the more determined to build on what he knows is a condemned foundation. The passionate energy with which *Heart of Darkness* exposes the shortcomings of imperialism is hardly consonant with nihilism, or terminal scepticism, nor is Conrad's belief in the need for sustaining illusions and his evident sympathy for Marlow's decision to lie to Kurtz's Intended.

Conrad's works are paradoxical and ambivalent, with the narrational and structural ironies frequently producing an alarming kind of deadlock. But while D.H. Lawrence said he could "never forgive Conrad for giving up on life", this is not fair. Some of Conrad's characters, like Decoud and

Razumov, do "give up", but only because they are forced into situations which they cannot survive. Marlow, however, never gives up. He does his lonely best to come to terms with a world he doesn't understand and he never loses his sense of decency. The alternative would be to surrender his humanity, and that – to recall the last words he speaks in *Heart of Darkness* – would be "too dark altogether".

A SHORT CHRONOLOGY

1857, December 3 Józef Teodor Konrad Korzeniowski born into a noble slightly impoverished family in the Polish Ukraine.

1861 His father, Apollo Korzeniowski, a playwright and translator, arrested on suspicion of plotting against Russian government and exiled to Vologda, a city 300 miles north of Moscow. His wife and son follow him into exile.

1865 Conrad's mother dies of tuberculosis.

1869 His father also dies of tuberculosis, leaving Conrad an orphan at the age of eleven. Placed in the care of his maternal uncle, Tadeusz Bobrowski, in Krakow.

1873 Conrad goes to Marseille to begin a career as a seaman.

1875-6 Sails twice to the West Indies; on the second voyage becomes friendly with the charismatic and swashbuckling first mate, Dominic Cervoni, almost certainly a gun-runner. On his return he is chided by his uncle for lack of prudence, having spent his three years' allowance in just two.

1878 Based in Marseille, loses all his money after investing in a risky and almost certainly illicit enterprise (involving contraband) and shoots himself in the chest with a revolver. His uncle puts out the story that he has been wounded in a duel. Conrad goes to England and begins going to sea in English ships. He also, he says, "began to learn English from East Coast chaps, each built to last for ever and coloured like a Christmas card".

1879 Sails up the Thames for the first time after a voyage to Australia in a clipper. The experience helped shape the famous opening scene of *Heart of Darkness*.

1886 Gains both his Master Mariner's certificate and British citizenship, officially changing his name to Joseph Conrad.

1890 Visits the Congo Free State as captain of the river steamer, Roi des Belges; the atrocities he witnesses inspire *Heart of Darkness*.

1894 Retires from the sea after 16 years in the Merchant Navy; meets Jessie George, his future wife. They have two sons, John and Borys.

1895 First novel, *Almayer's Folly*, is published.

1897-1911 Most productive phase of his career,

during which most of his major works published; lives in Essex, Bedfordshire and, for his last 15 years, in Kent, often off advances and state aid.

1913 Publication of *Chance,* which finally brings him popular success.

1924 Declines knighthood by Prime Minister Ramsay MacDonald. Dies at Bishopsbourne of a heart attack in August at the age of 67. Interred at Canterbury Cemetery.

BIBLIOGRAPHY

Achebe, Chinua, *An Image of Africa: Racism in Conrad's Heart of Darkness.* Original lecture at the University of Massachusetts, 1975. Reprinted in *Hopes and Impediments: Selected Essays by Chinua Achebe,* Doubleday, 1990

Brantlinger, Patrick, *Rule of Darkness: British Literature and Imperialism, 1830-1914,* Cornell University Press, 1988

Cunningham, Valentine, *In the Reading Gaol*, Blackwell, 1994

Fletcher, Chris, *Joseph Conrad*, The British Library, 1999

Forster, E.M., *Abinger Harvest*, Edward Arnold, 1940

Goonetilleke, D.C.R.A., *Joseph Conrad's Heart of Darkness*, Routledge, 2007

Kaplan, Carola; Mallios, Peter and White, Adrea (eds.), *Conrad in the Twenty-First Century*, Routledge, 2005

Lawrence, D.H. on Conrad and other authors, quoted in Scherr, Barry, *D.H. Lawrence Today: Literature, Culture and Politics*, Peter Lang, 2004

Leavis, F.R., *The Great Tradition*, first published 1948

Murfin, Ross, *Heart of Darkness: A Case Study in Contemporary Criticism*, St Martin's Press, 1989

Trilling, Lionel, *The Liberal Imagination*, 1950

Watts, Cedric, *A Preface to Conrad*, Longman, 1982

Watts, Cedric, *Joseph Conrad*, Northcote House, 1994

Watts, Cedric (ed.), *Joseph Conrad's Letters to R.B. Cunninghame Graham*, Cambridge University Press, 1969

Watt, Ian, *Essays on Conrad* (foreward by Frank Kermode), Cambridge University Press, 2000

INDEX

A

Achebe, Chinua 12, 19
"An Outpost of Progress" 20–22
Arrow of Gold, The 67

B

Bannerman, Helen
    Little Black Sambo 66
Beerbohm, Max
    A Christmas Garland 27
Blake 23
Brando, Marlon 64

C

Cary, Joyce 15
Chance 9, 110
Christie, Agatha
    Ten Little Niggers 47
Congo 43
Conrad in the Twenty-First
    Century 11, 16, 19
Conrad, Joseph
    Africa, depiction of 13–15
    British knighthood,
      declining 65
    Congo, time in 12
    critics 10–12
    England, coming to 64
    feminist assaults 29
    law, run-ins with 67
    major works 8–9
    paradoxical and
      ambivalent works of 124
    parody of 27
    pessimism 16–17, 86–87, 115
    picture of 37
    Roman Catholic, becoming 65
    self-indulgent negative whimsy,
      accusation of 33
    serial, works appearing in 67
    suicide, attempting 67
    view of the world,
      distinctive 113–125
Coppola, Francis Ford 5
    Apocalypse Now 41, 64, 91
Crusoe, Robinson 123
Cunningham, Valentine 33–35,
    88, 122, 123
    In The Reading Gaol, The 59

D

Dante
    Divine Comedy 39, 50, 100,
    102–103
Dostoevsky
    The Brothers Karamazov 61–62

E

Eliot, T.S. 4
    "Hollow Men, The" 40, 66, 100
    "La Fuiglia che Piange" 73
    Waste Land, The 64, 97 98,
    100
Eliot, George 115

F

Fin de Siècle 114–117
Forster, E.M.
    Abinger Harvest 26
    Passage to India, A 113–115
Fowler, H.W. 46
Freud 17, 117

G

Geertz, Clifford
  Islam Observed 82
"Geography and the Explorers" 12
Golding, William 4
Goonetilleke, D.C.R.A. 17, 122
Graham, Cunninghame 18, 34, 87, 115, 116, 121
Great Expectations 35, 36
Greene, Graham 4

H

Hardy, Thomas 86, 115, 117
Harlequin 59–61
Heart of Darkness
    American universities, studied in 18–19
    anti-imperialism 12–15
    completion of 4
    definite images 34–35
    depth and perspective 22
    Divine Comedy, comparative structure of 50, 102
    film adaptation 64
    flawed, considered as 26–38
    narrative failure 33–34
    narrative gap, no closure of 36
    plot, summary of 5–7
    preferred text 66
    primary narrator 24–26, 30–31
    progressive attitudes of 15
    racist, whether 12–16
    short novel, as 4
    subject matter of 10–19
    three parts, published in 4, 50
    works inspired by 64
Hughes, Ted 38–39
    Cave Birds 39

I

Ibsen
    The Wild Duck 121
India 14
Ivory 35

J

James, Henry 29–30, 32
Jane Eyre 35, 36, 38
Joyce, James 11, 30, 32
    Ulysses 11, 100

K

Karl, Frederick 34
Kermode, Frank 5
Kipling, Rudyard 16, 30
    Just So Stories 66
Klein, Georges Antoine 65
Kurtz
    background 13
    death and burial 9263
    influence for character of 65
    Marlow learning truth about 56–63
    Marlow putting faith in 50–56
    monster, as 61
    "The horror, the horror", meaning 84–96

L

Language, inadequacy of to represent reality 33
Lawrence, D.H. 29–32, 124
Leavis, F.R. 18, 27–38, 90
    D.H. Lawrence: Novelist 30
    Dickens, estimate of 30
    Great Tradition, The 28
Lennon, John 47
Leopold II of Belgium 12–13, 42,

Lord Jim 8, 81–84, 113, 124

M

Malkovich, John 64
Mann, Thomas
    Death in Venice 32
Marlow
    absurd, sense of 44
    breakdown 63, 96–102
    Brussels, in 40
    chain gang, seeing 45–47
    Company Director and doctor,
      meetings with 42–44
    Company Manager, meeting
      52–53
    Company's Outer Station,
      arrival at 45–47
    description of 36
    experiences in Africa 45–50
    first introduction of 22
    flaring up 21
    harlequin, meeting 59–61
    identification of Conrad with
      31–32
    importance of 20–26
    Intended, lying to 102–112
    journeys 79–84
    jungle, view of 68–74
    Kurtz, putting faith in 50–56
    Lord Jim, in 81–84
    mid-life crisis 39
    narrator and protagonist
      distinguished 35–36 reliving
      and revising story 22
    surreal humour 42
    time on Africa,
      life-changing nature of 38
    truth about Kurtz, learning
      56–63

    world of straightforward facts,
      breakdown of 38–50
    "Youth", in 22–23
Mid-life crisis 39
Miller, J. Hillis 16, 31, 68
Modernism 10

N

Nietzsche 16, 122
    Human, All Too Human 102,
      105-106
Nigger of the 'Narcissus' 46, 76,
    78, 87
Nigger, use of term 46–47
Nostromo 16, 75–76, 120

O

Orwell, George 15
Our Island Story 24

P

Pathetic fallacy 75–76
Potter, Beatrix
    Tale of Peter Rabbit, The 66

R

Racism 12–16, 19
Rom, Leon 65
Ruskin, John 75

S

Said, Edward 10–11, 16, 123
Secret Agent, The 9, 118
Singh, Francis 12
Stanley, Henry Morton 65
Stevenson, Robert Louis
    The Beach at Falesá 20, 68

T

Thiong'o. Ngugi wa 4

Trilling, Lionel 10, 17, 87
Twain, Mark 46, 96

U

Under Western Eyes 9, 120
Unwin, T. Fisher 20

W

Wagner
   The Ring 42
Warren, Robert Penn 109
Watt, Ian 62, 115, 121
Watts, Cedric 13, 17, 88–89
"Well Done" 55
Wells, H.G. 117
Welles, Orson 4
Wilde, Oscar
   Picture of Dorian Grey 117
Woolf, Leonard 15
   Village in the Jungle, The 68

Y

"Youth" 4, 8, 22–23, 39, 81

KEC LIBRARY NUNEATON CV11 4BE	
CLASS No.	BARCODE No.
823.912 BRA	